MW01487134

Abbie Burgess

LIGHTHOUSE HEROINE

Abbie Burgess

LIGHTHOUSE HEROINE

⚓

Ruth Sexton Sargent

AND

Dorothy Holder Jones

Copyright 1969 by Dorothy Holder Jones and Ruth Sexton Sargent
Published 1969 by Funk and Wagnalls, New York, NY
Paperback reprint 1976 by Downeast, Camden, Maine
Reprinted 1987 by Dorothy Holder Jones and Ruth Sexton Sargent
Reprinted 1996, 1997 by Lighthouse Digest, Wells, Maine

ISBN 0962 98825-1

To learn more about lighthouses, subscribe to *Lighthouse Digest,*
an international monthly lighthouse magazine.
Lighthouse Digest, PO Box 1690, Wells, Maine 04090.

ACKNOWLEDGMENTS

For their valuable assistance, we extend our grateful thanks to:

Miss Lysla Abbott, librarian of the Children's Room of the Portland Public Library, Portland, Maine.

Mrs. Pearl Dyer Davis of Peak's Island, Maine, whose father, Charles Dyer, was Keeper on Matinicus Rock, 1904–1908.

Thomas A. Jones of Falls Church, Virginia, who gave us technical advice.

Malcolm Leete of Peak's Island, Maine, who advised us about the customs, dress, and furniture of the era.

Mrs. Lois Marshall of South Portland, Maine, the great-granddaughter of Abbie Burgess Grant, who shared with us her letters and other mementoes of Abbie Burgess.

Norman Lee Sargent of Peak's Island, Maine, who served as our "marine consultant."

Mrs. Alvah B. Small, assistant librarian of the Maine Historical Society in Portland, Maine.

Edward Rowe Snow of Marshfield, Massachusetts, author and historian, who supplied us with much needed information.

D.H.J.
R.S.S.

*Dedicated, with deep affection,
to young readers everywhere.*

Contents

Authors' Note

From the moment we first heard of Abbie Burgess, we were enchanted with the story of her life. Abbie was only fourteen when she stepped upon Matinicus Rock that day in 1853, but she was no ordinary girl, for only a person with a special kind of strength could have endured the lonely life of tending lamps in a lighthouse.

Abbie's devotion to duty was matched by her courage. Accounts of her bravery during the great storms of 1856 and 1857 have been related in many books. In her own time, her name became a legend among seamen and throughout all of New England. We felt that such a heroine richly deserved a book of her own.

The major events in this story are true, and are as accurate as we could research and record them. However, scant material is available concerning some of the other members of the Burgess family and about a few of the happenings in Abbie's life, so we have depicted those people and events as we believe they might have been.

We learned that Samuel and Thankful Burgess had two daughters, Miranda and Louisa, before the birth of their son Benjy. These two girls remained on the mainland when the family went to Matinicus Rock, and there is reason to believe that one of them was married. A boy, Rufus, and another girl, Jane, were born after the young daughter named Mahala. Mr. and Mrs. Burgess must have felt it was much too precarious to take the two little babies to the Rock and therefore left them in the care of the older girls on the mainland. There are no records to show that these four children— Miranda, Louisa, Rufus, and Jane—played any part in the story of Abbie's years on Matinicus Rock.

The "rock birds" described in the book are a type of puffin noted for their brilliant plumage and clownlike antics. Matinicus Rock is the only place in North America where this particular breed of puffins may be found. Maine bird authorities believe that there were at least seventy pairs of puffins on the Rock in 1853. We doubt if the early lighthouse keepers knew what unusual birds they were. Today, however, every year in May, members of the Audubon Society make a special trip to the Rock to observe the puffins during their nesting time.

We have not exaggerated the difficulty of effecting the landing of a boat on Matinicus Rock. Even now, it requires great skill when the weather is *good;* when the ocean is rough, it defies the ablest of seamen. For this reason, the Coast Guard found it necessary, not too many years ago, to install a helicopter pad on the Rock, making it possible, in emergencies, for supplies to be flown in.

Abbie Burgess

LIGHTHOUSE HEROINE

Samuel Burgess Is Appointed Keeper

1 8 5 3

A GUST OF MARCH WIND rattled the kitchen shutters, tricking Abbie into thinking she heard her father's footsteps on the stoop outside. She hoped he'd return from his meeting at the Lighthouse Board before her sisters came back from their outing at the waterfront, for she had many questions to ask him.

All afternoon, while she'd been going about her housework, her mind had been busy wondering about the changes that would come into their lives if her father accepted the position of Keeper of the lighthouse on Matinicus Rock.

Until now, it had given her pleasure to think of living on one of the islands off the coast of Maine. It was as exciting to anticipate as a new book, with each day like a page she was waiting to read. But her mother had so many fears about the move that Abbie was obliged to consider them. Would her sisters, for instance, take to such a confining life? Would her brother, Benjy, be willing to live so far from the Rockland waterfront?

Most of her misgivings were for her mother, now asleep on the couch, weary from an afternoon of mending. Seeing her lying there under her afghan, with her gray hair braided about her head, her mother appeared to be even more frail, Abbie thought, than she rightly was.

Abbie had become resigned to the fact that her life was influenced by her mother's health. Whatever housework her mother was unable to do, fell to her, but she didn't mind that. She was tall, and strong for her age, and people often took her to be older than fourteen. But Abbie wondered now if living on the Rock would be too strenuous for her mother to bear.

She laid the petticoat she'd pressed on the stack of clothes atop the kitchen table, and set the iron back on the stove. As she picked up a piece of wood from the hearth, lifted one of the round lids on the stove, and dropped the wood inside, she tried to imagine how she herself would take to leaving Rockland.

Abbie set great store by the Ladies' Library, where she found so many poetry books to read. She'd miss the library, for sure. She knew she'd never be as popular as her friend, Prissy Pratt, but she'd miss the friends she'd made in Rockland. Abbie was certain that her light-brown hair, gray eyes, and rather ordinary features added up to plainness. Even so, she'd been invited to parties and church socials, and for afternoons of skating on the pond. But with her mother ill so much of the time, Abbie seldom went on outings now.

She had considered the practical side of her father's decision to apply for the position. Since she'd become responsible for most of the housework, much of the budgeting had been left to her. She knew what a struggle it was for him to support them all and buy medicine for her mother on the small salary he drew at the mill.

Abbie was stirring the chowder when she heard feet stamping in the entry off the kitchen. She slammed down the kettle lid and rushed to the door. Father was home!

With his dark beard and erect bearing, Abbie thought her father quite handsome, and though he was past fifty, his strength equaled that of a younger man. But at times, his quiet manner was irksome. She watched impatiently while he shook snow from his coat and cap and hung them on pegs in the entry.

"Father, what *happened?* Did you get the appointment?"

"Aye, Daughter." He followed her into the kitchen. Nodding at his wife who was waking from her nap, he said, "Let's tell your mother first. She's been anxious, too."

Mr. Burgess sat down on the couch and took his wife's hand in his. "It's all settled, Thankful. I filled out the necessary papers, and they swore me in. In just a few weeks, we'll be starting a new life."

"Oh, Sam," Mrs. Burgess responded, "it's so uncertain. All you know about that job, that Rock, is what you've been told. We don't know what it's really like out there. We'll be shut off from everything, from everyone——"

"We won't be isolated, Thankful. We'll be free! They tell me it's warmer on the Rock in winter than it is on the mainland, and cooler in the summer. And the salt air is so invigorating that you're bound to get well and strong."

"But my medicine, and our food—and how will the children go to school?"

Abbie took cornmeal from the cupboard and began mixing johnnycake batter, listening all the while as her father explained that the Rock was only twenty-two miles out from Rockland and six miles from Matinicus Island.

"So long's the weather's good, Ben and I can get food and other things from the mainland. The government supply boat comes out once a month—weather permitting—with mail and oil for the lamps. We'll teach the girls at home. Abbie hasn't been to school in nearly a year, but she's as smart with figures as Ben, and a heap better at reading."

His voice grew gentle as he went on, "Change is always uncertain, Thankful, but it's a challenge. You know I've had a mind to be my own boss. I've tried fishing and farming and mill work. At my age, it's high time I dropped anchor and stayed put."

The clatter of footsteps in the entry interrupted his words. Nine-year-old Esther burst into the kitchen, her brown hair glistening with snow, her gray eyes sparkling.

"Father," she blurted, "did they give you the position?"

Mr. Burgess had no sooner replied than eight-year-old Mahala darted in and past her sister, her blond hair tossing about. "He got it, he got it! Father's going to be a lighthouse!"

"A lighthouse *keeper*," eleven-year-old Lydia corrected her. "And go hang up your wraps where they belong. You're scattering snow all over the floor!" Her reddish hair gleamed in the lamplight. She smiled in pleasure. "How soon are we moving, Father?"

Before Mr. Burgess commenced explanations, Benjy came home. Abbie could hardly wait to hear her brother's reaction to the news. He was nearly seventeen, but full grown in many ways.

"Mr. Pratt didn't need me any longer today," Benjy remarked as he joined them. "He's closing the store early." He brushed back his thick sandy-brown hair and eyed them anxiously. "Well, what happened today?"

Mahala skipped over to her brother. "Father's going to keep a lighthouse. We'll all be living out in the ocean."

Benjy put more wood on the fire, backed his lanky frame up to it, and warmed his hands. "So we're moving out to that Rock. Well, if you won't mind a few storms, Father, I reckon we won't."

"That's enough, Son. There's no point stirring up fear in your mother and sisters."

Mrs. Burgess leaned forward. "What's this about storms, Sam?"

Abbie went to her mother. "Don't let Benjy frighten you, Mother. He's referring to that storm in 1827 that washed away the towers on the Rock. But it was one of the worst storms the coast has ever seen."

Mrs. Burgess nodded thoughtfully. "Mercy—I'd forgotten that happened on Matinicus Rock!" She glanced at Mr. Burgess. "Sam, what are you getting us into?"

He patted her hand. "Thankful, the same storm that hit the Rock, hit here at Rockland, too. The new towers on the Rock are granite, and so's the house. They'll be standing long after we're gone."

Esther came over to the couch and hugged her mother. "*I'm* not afraid, Mother. I want to live on the Rock, even if a storm *does* come. All of us do."

Mrs. Burgess smoothed Esther's brown hair. "I'm a great hand at worrying. I suppose it's just my nature." She smiled at them fondly. "What would I do without my dear family?"

Suddenly Benjy straightened up. "I smell something burning, Sis."

"Sakes' alive!" Abbie pulled the johnnycake from the oven just in time.

Esther came up beside her, and dipped a finger into the chowder. "The johnnycake looks delicious, Abbie. Want me to sample it?"

"I'd rather you helped Lydia set the table. Mahala, put clean napkins into the rings. And, Benjy—the firewood is getting low."

On the way out to the shed, Benjy lifted the kettle lid and sniffed the chowder. "You're a good cook, Abbie. One of these days some fellow's going to throw a net over you and haul you in. But if we move to that Rock, it'll have to be a shipwrecked sailor, and *you'll* do the catching."

Abbie enjoyed being teased by her brother, but not about the Rock. "Father," she asked now, "we will get to visit Rockland now and then, won't we?"

Mr. Burgess nodded. "Aye, Daughter." He settled Mrs. Burgess in the kitchen chair nearest the warm fire. "The Rock will mean even more work for you, I fear. You'll have to keep a close haul on the girls, while Benjy and I keep the lights burning."

Abbie sliced the johnnycake. "I won't mind the work, Father. Not many girls have the chance to live on a lighthouse station. It should be a great adventure."

She poured the chowder into the large tureen, set the other dishes around, and the family sat down at the round, pine table.

Heads bowed while Mr. Burgess asked a blessing. Then he

ladled the chowder into soup plates for Mrs. Burgess and the girls. He served Benjy next, and himself last of all.

"I can hardly wait to see the Rock," Lydia declared. "There's bound to be a lot to draw out there. Last summer, down at the waterfront, I tried to sketch the ocean—but it never looked just right."

Esther gave a wistful sigh. "Benjy will get to fish, Lydia will draw pictures, and Mahala will explore everything. And Abbie will sit and watch the ocean. But what can I do, Father? There won't be anything for *me* to do."

Mr. Burgess chuckled. "You'll be busy sampling all the new foods. Why, there's fish we've never tried before swimming in the ocean near that Rock. And all of you can fly kites, and raise and lower the flag—on days the weather's good. The lighthouse is government property, so there's a flagpole, and part of our duty will be to fly Old Glory whenever we're able."

Mahala spoke up now, "Father, is the light one great big candle? How will you keep the wind from blowing it out?"

The others laughed heartily at Mahala's imagination.

"Not one big candle, Mahala," her father replied. "There are two light towers with fourteen lamps in each. Every evening at sunset, Benjy and I will light twenty-eight lamps. Every morning at sunrise, we'll snuff them out. The wind can't blow them out, because they're inside the tower with glass windows all around. They tell me the beams of Matinicus Light can be seen for fifteen miles on a clear night."

"Matinicus," Lydia repeated, as if testing the word on her tongue. "I'll never learn to spell *that*."

"It's from the Indian word 'Manasquesicook,'" Mr. Burgess explained, "which means a collection of grassy islands.

But this island didn't get its share of grass. It's a reef of barren rock, the farthest lighted point on the rockbound coast of Maine. It's a solemn trust to keep the lights tended. People's lives and property will depend on my doing the job right."

Mahala was still curious. "Father, why do the ships *need* a lighthouse?"

"Because of the rocks. The shoreline of Maine has a lot of reefs that jut out in unexpected places. Parts of them are visible to seamen, but the larger part is usually hidden under water. A ship could run aground on a reef and be destroyed. In fact, a great many were before that lighthouse was built."

Abbie had become so intrigued by the conversation that she hadn't noticed until now that Benjy was scowling. Wasn't he pleased about the Rock, with all its opportunities for fishing? But what he thought about their move wouldn't matter too much, she reflected, for in a few years he'd leave home to make his own way. That reminded Abbie of one of her questions.

"Father, how long do you figure you'll be Keeper?"

"It's a political appointment, so as long as the Democrats are in office, the job is secure. I'll have to be reappointed each year, though."

He took a slip of paper from his shirt pocket. "The salary is four hundred and fifty dollars a year—same amount the first keeper was paid twenty-five years ago. This list is the quarterly allowance the government furnishes each keeper. Assistants gets it, too. In time, I hope to get Benjy appointed as my assistant. He'd be paid three hundred dollars a year, and get the allowance, to boot."

He read aloud, "Forty pounds of salt pork, fifty-two

pounds of salt beef, one hundred pounds of flour, eighty pounds of chip biscuits, eleven and one-half pounds brown sugar, six pounds of coffee or one and one-half pounds tea, five pounds of rice, and two gallons beans or peas."

He folded the paper. "Those staples will keep us well fed for three months, Thankful. And with the fish Ben catches, and other food we haul out from the mainland, we'll get along right well."

Mrs. Burgess smiled wanly. "Sam, I can see the advantages of the move. But we've made so many changes—how can I know this one will be any better? I'll do my part keeping the accounts, and I'll make a list of things we'll be needing. We should take enough provisions to tide us over until you come back to the mainland again."

Abbie's father looked relieved. "You're a good, brave woman, Thankful. Once you get that salt air in your lungs, and the sun on your face, you'll feel as spry as Abbie." He handed Benjy the last of the johnnycake. "The house is partly furnished, like this one. Just make sure the girls take plenty to keep them occupied until we come back for the rest of our belongings."

Abbie's spirits soared when her mother said, "Benjy, you may bring the trunks down from the attic for us, so we womenfolk can start packing. Girls, we'll have to tidy this house for the next tenant."

Lydia sighed. "I hoped we'd be gone before we'd have to clean again."

"We won't do much spring cleaning," her mother assured her. "The move will be demanding enough. We'll just sort out things as we pack; then, before we leave, we'll go over the rooms and smarten them up."

After supper, Abbie and her sisters spent a lively hour tending to their evening chores. Once the kitchen table was cleared, the girls brought out their handiwork. Lydia embroidered her rose-garden sampler; Esther let out the hem of one of Mahala's dresses; and Abbie whipped in the hem of another one. While the girls' hands were busy, their mother called out words for them to spell. After that, they worked sums on their slates, and took turns reading aloud from McGuffey's Reader.

"You'd best take your pressed-flower collection," Abbie told Lydia after a while, "and your crayons and drawing paper. Be sure to bring along the sampler that says 'God Bless Our Happy Home.' "

Esther looked up from her slate. "Don't forget our jelly, Abbie, and the meat hanging in the shed."

"And our books," Mahala put in. "And my blue dress and new shoes."

Mr. Burgess was sitting by the fire reading the newspaper. "Girls, don't pack your ice skates or sleds. Mr. Pratt will keep them for us in a back shed. We'll have no use for them on the Rock."

The girls exchanged glances. "Doesn't it snow out on the Rock?" Mahala blurted.

"We'll have a lot of snow out there," Abbie replied. "So we'd best take our snowshoes. Father only means there won't be any frozen ponds to skate on, or hills to slide down. But there'll be other things to enjoy."

Study time over, the girls dressed for bed, then gathered at the table for the nightly Bible reading. Afterward, Mrs. Burgess led the younger ones upstairs to bed. Abbie sat on at the kitchen table, mending by the lamplight, listening to her father tell Benjy about a lighthouse keeper's duties, and the splendid dark blue uniform with silver buttons he'd be wearing on special occasions.

Abbie could tell that her father was proud he'd been chosen for a position of such responsibility and prestige. She hoped that his yearning for the sea would be satisfied now.

Keeping house and caring for her younger sisters had become Abbie's role in life. She'd never expected more than this, nor had she dared hope for more. Her favorite diversion, whenever she could snatch an hour for herself, was to walk by the sea.

Now, she thought, there would be a purpose in her life beyond housekeeping, for it would surely be a challenge just to live on Matinicus Rock.

Preparations for Departure

ABBIE STOOD at the kitchen table wrapping jars of jellies and preserves in newspapers, while she listened to Priscilla Pratt carry on about an evening of ice skating on the lake under a full moon. Prissy's words were getting as fancy as her clothes, Abbie noticed. Her new blue woolen coat and matching bonnet had been ordered all the way from New York.

"And on the ride home," Prissy confided, "Thad raced his sleigh with Jed Tobias—you know how reckless they are. Mama would be furious if she knew!" Her golden curls bounced about with every turn of her head.

"But I didn't come to talk about myself," she hurried on. "I want to know if you're really and truly going to the Rock. The girls were gossiping about it at school today. They said if *their* father took such a job, they'd refuse to go. They'd much rather stay in Rockland with friends. Abbie, you could share my room——"

"But my heart's set on going, Prissy. Father *needs* me. He couldn't manage without me."

Prissy smiled. "I told the girls you'd jump at the chance to have your own sailboat, and get all brown and leathery sitting out in the sun." She let out a sigh. "I declare, I couldn't give up parties and sleigh rides—and beaus."

"You know I've never cared about parties and beaus, Prissy." She glanced at her two younger sisters who were helping her pack the preserves. "If I stayed here, I'd miss my sisters even more." She held up a jar of blackberry jam. "We spent hours in the woods together picking the berries for these."

Prissy picked up one of the jars. "You're so domestic, Abbie. And I recognize Lydia's artistic touch on the labels. There's a blackberry sketched on this one—and this must be a blueberry."

The younger girls had been listening keenly to the conversation. When Mahala came over and set another jar beside Abbie, she blurted, "Prissy, don't you fret about Abbie. She'll have plenty of beaus. Benjy said there'd be some shipwrecked sailors on the Rock."

Abbie gasped, and Prissy burst into giggles. "Very well, Mahala," Prissy said, "I won't mind about the beaus. But I'll still worry about all of you out there surrounded by miles and miles of ocean———"

Benjy stepped into the kitchen in time to retort, "And tons and tons of fish!" Stopping in front of Prissy, he bowed with a flourish. "How fetching you look today, Miss Pratt!"

"You never stop, do you, Benjy Burgess?"

Their joking enlivened the visit so much that Abbie wondered how they would all bear the loss of their friends. Would the companionship of sisters and a brother be enough out on the Rock?

Presently, Prissy got to her feet. "I must go, Abbie. Dinner's at six, and Thad's calling for me at seven. I do wish you would come tonight. Rebecca's parties are such fun."

"I couldn't go without an escort. And the girls and I have to wash our hair tonight. With four of us, that's a chore."

Prissy looked sad now. "I clear forgot to ask—when are you leaving?"

"In about two weeks. Father's going out on the supply boat day after tomorrow and stay a spell at the lighthouse, so the present Keeper can show him how to perform his duties. He'll come back in a dory and leave it at the wharf until we're ready to sail."

Prissy touched her arm. "Will you get to the mainland very often?"

Abbie shrugged. "Father and Benjy will take turns coming back for supplies. But if they're ever gone at the same time, I just might get a chance to take charge. Unless Mother's health improves a great deal, I won't be leaving the Rock often."

After word got around, neighbors and friends dropped in to speculate about the Burgesses' new life, and gradually Abbie's mother lost some of her fears about the dangers of living on the Rock. Most people were of the opinion that their move was well worth risking a few storms.

When Mr. Burgess returned from his visit to Matinicus Light Station, the family greeted him with joy. But Abbie held her breath as they joined hands around the supper table that evening. Please, Father, she wanted to say, if it's going to be hard for all of us there—don't tell us!

Mr. Burgess rubbed his beard, but there was a twinkle in his dark eyes. "Wait 'til you see that house, family. It's right in the center of the Rock, with no neighbors crowding it. It's like no other place I've ever been—with the sea, the sky, and the gulls." He turned to Mrs. Burgess. "There's a fine cistern, and a pump in the kitchen. If the salary and food allowance aren't enough, the Keeper allowed we could do some lobstering."

Benjy, hunched over his plate, said glumly, "Lobstering. My idea of fishing is being way out there on the deep water, not hauling up a mess of lobster traps. Father, I heard about a fleet of boats the other day—they're taking on new men."

Mr. Burgess was frowning. "Ben, your place is at the lighthouse with me. There's enough work there to keep two men busy around the clock. But I reckon you can fit in a little fishing trip now and then."

Abbie felt relieved when Benjy replied, "Yes, Father."

The next morning, she awoke with a happy heart. A whole new life was awaiting them—in only a few weeks. As she did her chores, she discussed the move with her mother. To her dismay, Mother said, "I can see what's coming, Abigail. Benjy will up and leave, your father will overwork himself, and I'll be sick with worry. Your father's gone adrift this time, for sure."

"Oh, Mother, we don't rightly know what Benjy will do— or what it'll be like on the Rock. Father's feeling so proud. And the girls are so excited they can hardly eat."

Her mother nodded. "That's because they're young and have their health. They haven't weathered the hard times I have. That reminds me—my bottle of tonic is nearly empty.

Will you run down to the pharmacist's for me? On the way back, you can stop at Mr. Pratt's and buy some supplies. Benjy can haul them home on the sled."

Abbie quickly agreed. She was anxious to leave before her mother thought of any more reasons why the move was wrong for them. She put on her warm, high-topped shoes, buttoned up her heavy woolen coat, and wrapped a shawl about her head.

The March wind had a bite in it, but Abbie didn't mind. No matter how weary she was, the tang of sea air lifted her spirits. She scuffed along the cobblestone street heading for the shops on the waterfront, savoring every sight and smell and sound.

She peered at the windows of shops and read every sign. There was one of her favorites: "Elias Crane—Importer of china, porcelain, tea, and all manner of delicacies from the Far East."

On the corner she stopped in front of a placard posted on a building. "Twenty able-bodied seamen needed at once for the *Sophia Maria*. Fastest ship afloat. Good wages, good meals. Ports-of-call North Africa, Canary Islands, San Francisco, and Hong Kong. We sail with the tide on Wednesday."

Why, that's today, she realized. She walked on, mulling over how thrilling it must be to be a man, to venture around the world, visit exotic cities, meet strange people. Though the announcement made the work sound alluring, and most ships were commanded by respectable captains, others were notorious for their hardships. Hellships, they were called. Only men who were desperate ever signed on a hellship.

As she reached the waterfront, she thought how right the

Indians were in naming Rockland "Cutawamkeg," which meant Great Landing Place, for indeed it was.

Three clipper ships were standing in the harbor now, their masts reaching toward the sky. Large crates were being swung from the booms overhead and carefully lowered to the ground, where crews were waiting to haul them into warehouses. Abbie wished she could peek inside the crates. Did they contain silks, elegant furniture, or fancy things from the Orient? Now and then, when she visited the waterfront, a ship would be loading a cargo of trees that had been cut from Maine woods and floated downstream to the wharves, destined to become masts for ships of the English navy.

All along the waterfront there were spacious homes with "widow walks" on their roofs—small areas fenced in by railings. In good weather, a seaman's wife could climb up to a widow's walk and search the horizon with a telescope for a glimpse of a ship coming into port. Nearly every ship that sailed in bore messages of other ships sighted and passed during the voyage. Such news passed quickly through the town.

After she'd bought the bottle of tonic, she hurried up the street, eager to visit Mr. Pratt's store with its curios from all over the world. There were glass-topped counters holding native handiwork from Samoa, and shelves stacked with fine fabrics from various countries. The pressed ferns were Lydia's favorites, and Prissy never tired of telling Abbie about the latest dresses that had arrived from Paris.

In the sundry section of the store, Abbie called off the staples her mother had written on the list. She bought more embroidery and samplers for Esther and Mahala, some drawing paper for Lydia, as well as starch, clothespins, matches, and other household articles.

Instead of Benjy using a sled, Mr. Pratt allowed him to haul the merchandise home in his horse-drawn wagon. Benjy loaded up, then lifted Abbie onto the front seat beside him.

Abbie closed her eyes, letting the cold wind whip against her face, blow her long hair about. She took advantage of their privacy and said to Benjy, "Please don't speak again about leaving home when Mother's around. She was doing so much better. But after last night—after you spoke of wanting to join a fishing fleet—she's upset about the move." Abbie knew her words wouldn't take well with Benjy, but she had to say them.

"Sis, I'm glad Father got the appointment and didn't let Mother talk him out of accepting it. But it doesn't change my feelings. I'm nearly seventeen, old enough to go my own way. Father wants to set me on that Rock, make me keep those lights burning—when I'd rather be out there, rocked by the waves and with the lights burning *for* me."

Abbie remembered the announcement of the sailing of the *Sophia Maria*. She was obliged to make Benjy see how much the family needed him now. She finished her speech with, "Do give Father time to get us settled before you go away."

Benjy stared ahead. "I'll try to be patient, but I can't promise how long I'll stay on the Rock."

"Benjy, if you'll help Father and not upset Mother now, I'll side with you—when the right time comes."

CHAPTER III

Sailing to Matinicus Rock

ABBIE'S FATHER had agreed to take over the lighthouse station on the second Tuesday in April, 1853. Abbie and her
mother planned the chores so well that all was in readiness
the evening before their departure. At the close of their Bible
reading, Mr. Burgess led them in a prayer for a safe and
pleasant journey.

Abbie was awakened at dawn the next morning by the
sound of her father building a fire in the kitchen stove. Then
she heard him leave to get the hired sleigh and horse at Mr.
Pratt's store. Abbie awakened the others and coaxed them
into tending to the chores they'd each been assigned.

In the kitchen, she fried slices of cold cornmeal mush,
with slices of apple and salt pork, in the spider—the three-
legged skillet. She had breakfast ready to serve by the time
her father returned.

"We can be at the wharf within the hour," he told them,
"if you girls will clear the kitchen while Ben and I load up
the sleigh." He helped himself to a large serving from every

dish. "Clean up those plates, children. There'll be a cold wind blowing, and you'll be glad you've got something warm in your stomachs."

The girls washed and dried the dishes, then packed them while their mother filled the lunch basket. As they were bustling about, Mrs. Stevens, who lived next door, appeared with a plate of ginger cookies.

"I saw you getting under way, Thankful, so I came to say good-by."

The visit was cut short when Mr. Burgess told them it was time to set out. Abbie picked up the lunch basket, and her father carried the water jug as he closed the door behind them.

Outside, Mahala and Esther were dancing about. "Look what I found!" Mahala exclaimed. "A pussy willow! It was poking out through the snow!" She waved it about for all to see.

"Hold onto it, little one," Mr. Burgess said. "There'll be no flowers on the Rock for you to pick."

Though it was not yet seven o'clock, many townspeople were up and about. Abbie was saddened to think how long it might be before she saw houses again, or heard the clop-clop-ping of horses' hoofs, or the sound of the bell in the church steeple tolling the hour. Until her father mentioned it, she'd never noticed how close together the houses were, or how the smoke from the lime kilns settled in a haze over the roofs. She'd never taken to the peculiar odor of the smoke. Some people thought it purified the air and prevented epidemics. She was glad they were getting away from it. It would be a pleasure to breathe the pure sea air on the Rock.

After the dory was filled with their belongings, Mr. Burgess took his wife's arm. "Come along, Thankful—we should get started."

As Abbie stepped down into the dory, she glanced back for a last look at the town spread along the waterfront. Just then she spied a girl running toward them, her blond curls streaming out from under a red scarf.

"It's Prissy!" Abbie cried.

Benjy looked up. "She's got a package—probably a present for you. If I know Prissy, it'll be something you can't use on the Rock."

"Abbie," Prissy explained breathlessly, as she handed the package down to Benjy, "I wanted to give you something to remember me by!"

"Oh, Prissy, thank you," Abbie called back. "I'll write you often, and I'll come visit whenever I can!"

"Fred," Benjy shouted to a young friend who was standing on the wharf, "cast off!"

Fred untied the boat, and tossed the end of the rope down to Benjy, who pushed his hands against the wharf, shoving the boat out into the water.

"Have a good trip!" Fred yelled.

Abbie sat down next to Mahala on one of the center seats. They all waved good-by to Prissy. "Prissy!" Benjy called, "if you ever hanker to go fishing, come out to the Rock!"

Prissy grimaced. Abbie and Benjy chuckled, for they both knew how much she loathed fishing.

The trunks and wooden barrels had been snugly stowed amidships, where Benjy now sat to tend the sail. After Mrs. Burgess had been comfortably settled against a pile of bedding in the bow, Mr. Burgess took his place at the tiller in the stern. He'd been given the bearings on the course to

Matinicus Rock, and with a dependable compass to guide them, they were on their way at last.

The younger girls were entranced with the gulls that wheeled above them, but finally they settled down in their places in the bow, huddling against one another.

Sitting across from Abbie, Lydia shivered. "I don't set much store by sailing. The wind stings my face, and the water sprays me."

"You'll get used to it," Abbie told her. She tugged a blanket from the pile at her feet and handed it to Lydia. "Here—tuck this around you and Esther and you won't notice the chill so much."

She wrapped another blanket around Mahala's legs, and then her own. Even with their coats, mittens, and mufflers, they felt the sharp wind.

Mahala looked up and asked, "When do you reckon we'll get to the Rock?"

Benjy answered first. "With the wind in our favor, we'll be there about supper time." He glanced up at the sail. "See? Instead of a horse pulling us along, the wind is pushing against the sail—taking us where we've a mind to go." He leaned back, contentedly. "After these waves rock you a while, you'll forget the cold."

Finally settled, Abbie opened the package Prissy had given her. Her sisters leaned closer as she lifted the lid, uncovering a pink comb, brush, and mirror set. It was made of wood and had a dainty flower design on the back of the mirror and brush.

Lydia was awed. "It surely came from Paris, Abbie. I've seen some like it at Mr. Pratt's store."

"It's just what you'll need, Sis. A comb and brush to un-

tangle your wind-blown hair, and a mirror to see how well
you did it," Benjy said teasingly.

Mahala tugged at Abbie's sleeve. "Look———" She pointed
toward the mainland. "The houses are getting smaller and
smaller. Does that mean we're getting bigger and bigger?"

Abbie laughed. "No, Mahala. We're just sailing farther
away. Look at the hills behind Rockland—they'll soon be just
a speck on the horizon."

Huddled close and warm under their blankets, the girls
were soon lulled to sleep. Mrs. Burgess dozed, too. Abbie
pulled the edge of the blanket close around her shoulders.
The cold wind and the lift of the boat as it plunged through
the water exhilarated her.

She closed her eyes for a moment to listen to the water rush
and spill. Then she heard her father talking in a low voice to
Benjy. "Son, I couldn't let on to your mother how concerned
the officer at the Lighthouse Board was about appointing me
Keeper, in view of my family circumstances. He doubted I
could manage the work and care for my family, with no help
to call on. But I set his mind at rest when I told him I had a
son near grown. Once you've mastered the lamps, Ben, I
know that if an emergency arose, I could leave the Rock
without feeling uneasy."

Abbie held her breath until Benjy replied, "You can count
on me, Father. I know the job means a good deal to all of
you. I don't hold to Mother and the girls living out so far,
but they should be safe enough in a granite house."

"Son, I believe we'll fare as well there as on the mainland.
Keeping the job depends on the political climate, and there's
nothing I can do about that."

There was a long silence and then Benjy said, "Father, I'll

do my part, but in my opinion, Abbie could tend those lights same as I could."

Abbie sat still, certain those words would rile their father.

"Abbie has her work, Son, and the lighthouse is *our* work. I can't fathom you, Ben. The rest of us admire to call that island our own, but not you."

"Father, not even a lighthouse can change my feelings about fishing," Benjy insisted. "Dropping a line's the most exciting life there is! You're always wondering—how many fish will I lure to my line? When will the big one come along? Will I outsmart him and haul him in, or will he trick me and get away? The sea's teeming with life, ready to match wits with you. And there's no lack of work. Why, I hear tell of crews signing up every day——"

"Fishermen will never lack for work around these parts, but it's a hard life. I spent more years in a boat than I'd care to count."

Hearing men talk about fishing had always been part of Abbie's life. The waters off the coast of Maine were rich with flounder, mackerel, cod, and halibut, so the fishing industry provided a livelihood for many families. Abbie remembered when her father sailed away one year with other men from Matinicus Island to fish off the Grand Banks near Canada.

Last year, after the Burgesses moved to Rockland, and he'd found work at Mr. Pratt's store near the waterfront, Benjy was full of talk about the trading vessels that brought supplies from England and Europe. He kept track of the coasters that stopped at Rockland on their way to transport commodities down to other large seaports on the Atlantic Coast.

Once, when times were hard, Abbie's father considered signing for work on a lime boat. Because of the danger of water leakage, which might seep into the lime and cause it to heat, expand, and possibly explode, wages on lime boats were much higher. But that wasn't long after Mahala was born, and Mrs. Burgess didn't feel strong enough to look after all the children alone.

Benjy was a sturdy lad by the age of twelve, so he'd picked up jobs whenever he could. During the winter months, he often worked at warehouses that stored blocks of ice after they had been sawed from the frozen lakes and rivers. Benjy's duty was to lift the blocks down from the wagons, stack them, and cover them with sawdust to keep them from melting. A ship's hold filled with ice represented an inexpensive cargo that reaped large profits in the Southern Hemisphere, so there were many firms in the Rockland area that stored and transported ice.

"Abbie," her father suddenly shouted, "we have some escorts!" He pointed. "Look there—seals!"

"Seals!" She peered across the expanse of gray water until she spied a shiny black hump. She shook the younger girls awake, and they peeked over their blankets, chuckling as two baby seals rounded up out of the waves, then rolled down beneath them.

"They're following us along," Benjy said. "Watch up ahead now; they'll be coming up again."

One little seal emerged and swam near the dory for several minutes. Then it rounded over and disappeared again.

After a while, Mrs. Burgess brought out the lunch basket. The younger girls shoved to get closer, begging for extra portions of food before they'd even been served.

Mr. Burgess was amused. "There's nothing like sea air to whet the appetite."

Bread and cheese had never been so tasty, and Mrs. Stevens' ginger cookies pleased everyone.

"Throw your scraps out in the water, children," their father told them, "and watch the gulls come after them."

Esther collected a napkinful of scraps and hurled them over the side. Instantly, the gulls swooped down to the water.

"You can see why they're called the scavengers of the sea," Mr. Burgess told them. "They eat whatever they find on the water's surface."

Abbie passed around the hard candy, and it soon disappeared. When the girls grew restless, Mrs. Burgess suggested, "Esther, why don't you sing for us? The wind isn't blowing quite so hard now, and we should hear you well."

Esther ducked her head. "I can't sing by myself."

"*I'll* sing!" Mahala volunteered. "Oh, blow the man down, bullies, blow the man down! To me, way-aye, blow the man down!"

Lydia and Abbie gasped in shock, and Esther giggled. Mr. Burgess rubbed his beard, but Mrs. Burgess frowned. "Mahala," she demanded, "where did you ever hear *that?*"

Mahala pointed to her brother. "Benjy sings it when he does his chores."

"Well, young ladies don't sing sea chanteys. Esther, you should know all the words to 'Blest Be the Tie That Binds.' Let's hear that one."

Esther began to sing in a clear sweet tone, gracing the air with the familiar melody. Over her shyness now, she led the family in other hymns. They sang with such gusto that Benjy remarked, "This sounds like the seamen's Sunday service back in Rockland."

Before long, Abbie's mother and sisters fell asleep again.

Abbie felt drowsy enough to sleep, but she couldn't bear to miss the moment of their arrival. She would close her eyes for a spell, then open them, straining for a glimpse of an island with a lighthouse on it.

Suddenly, a large gray mound appeared on the horizon. "Father," she cried, rubbing her eyes, "is that the Rock?"

"Aye! We have quite a ways to go, but the wind's picking up now."

Benjy teased her about her eagerness, but Abbie paid him no heed. She fixed her eyes on the mound, and it gradually took the shape of a large rock rising out of the ocean.

"You can see the roof of the house from here," her father called back. "And see the towers at each end."

"I can't figure why they built *two* towers," Benjy remarked. "Seems to me one would have been trouble enough."

Mr. Burgess shrugged. "I can't fathom it, either, unless it's the fog up here. One light may not be bright enough during fog."

Lydia stirred, then jerked her head up. "Are we there?"

"Nearly." Abbie pointed toward the Rock. "Look there——"

Lydia's squeal of surprise aroused Esther and Mahala, who blinked at the sight ahead with large, curious eyes.

Gulls had soared over them from time to time since they'd set sail, and now these were joined by terns. As they neared the Rock, the girls spotted several strange-looking birds with bright bills. Several of them were walking about upon the ledge above.

"The Keeper called those colorful ones 'rock birds,' " Mr. Burgess told them. "They're clowns, too, if you take the time to watch them."

"Mercy, what a welcoming committee!" Mrs. Burgess exclaimed. "All those gulls lined up on that ledge, staring down at us. And that must be their scouting party circling above, looking over the new tenants."

Esther clamped her hands over her ears. "They're so *noisy!* Are they telling us to go away?"

"They're always noisy," Mr. Burgess replied. "There's no chance to get lonely on an island with these creatures around."

He began to explain the landing procedure. "There's only one safe landing spot on the Rock, and even that's treacherous in rough weather. A little cove beyond this place could be used for a landing, but it would be my second choice—no matter what the weather."

He began to reef the sail and lower the mast. "Grab the oars now, Ben. There's a real trick to riding a boat in. I learned it when I came out here. You're obliged to wait until a wave is just right, and row in on its crest. Then, a man has to jump on land, hang onto the rope, and wait until a good wave comes along to haul the boat in." He shook his head. "I can't figure how a man could land a boat alone here without doing some damage to it."

Right in the midst of all this, Mahala asked eagerly, "Father, does this boat belong to us?"

"Aye, little one. Long as we're here, it'll be ours."

Esther caught Mahala's enthusiasm. "Can we name it, Father?"

"Aye. Whatever suits your fancy."

The girls chattered among themselves, then consulted Benjy and Abbie. Finally, Mrs. Burgess interrupted them. "I think it should rightly be called *Provider*. It'll surely be that while we're here."

Mr. Burgess asked for their close attention. "Now, remember," he warned them, "if anyone stands up suddenly, we'll all have a ducking. So just sit quietly until it's your turn to climb out."

The womenfolk waited in silence while the men pulled on the oars, skillfully bringing the dory to the edge of the landing site. The boat crunched on the rock surface beneath it. Benjy jumped ashore with the rope and hauled on it until the *Provider* was snug in the ways—the wooden planks placed in the narrow inlet to keep boats above the incoming tide.

Mr. Burgess lifted Lydia out first and carried her over to the stairlike formation of rock just above the water. After the women were ashore, they waited on the ledge above while Benjy and Mr. Burgess pulled the dory up to a more firmly docked position in the ways.

Finally, all together, the Burgesses began the long walk up toward the house.

CHAPTER IV

Arrival at the Lighthouse

"THERE IT IS," Mr. Burgess said, as they beheld the acres of barren rocks and the house in the distance. "That house may be the heart of the island, but the lights in those towers will be the brain. Whatever else we do, we're obliged to keep them burning."

While her sisters skipped ahead, Abbie walked slowly, relishing the sight of it all.

Benjy stamped along beside her, grumbling, "What's so beautiful about this place? Not a tree or a blade of grass. Just gray rock as far as you can see—thirty-two acres of it!"

"Oh, Benjy, what does that matter? Doesn't all this space and sky lift your spirits? Listen to the waves! And smell the fresh, salty air. I'm so proud that we've been chosen to be 'Guardians of the Coast.' There's the flagpole Father spoke about—with Old Glory waving a greeting. There just couldn't be another place in all the world as exciting as this!"

After they passed the boathouse, Mr. Burgess pointed out the various wooden sheds scattered about. The small cobblestone dwelling, he explained, was one of the first buildings on the Rock, and it was now used as a wash house.

"We have a lot to store here," he told them. "Whale oil for the lamps, ropes, lobster traps, and a spare boat. Everything on the Rock must be fastened down in foul weather, or it could be washed clear out to sea." Glancing at his wife, he quickly added, "Don't fret, Thankful. You're about to see for yourself that our new home isn't likely to wash away."

Mahala darted ahead of them, shouting, "A bell, a bell!"

"That must be the fog bell," Benjy said.

Some distance behind the house stood a structure of four wooden poles and framework, all painted white. In the center hung a huge bell, green from corrosion. Mr. Burgess explained that the bell weighed a ton, and the poles were cemented deep into the rock in order to support the weight.

"Now, children," he warned, "don't get under that bell when it's ringing, or it'll deafen you for hours. The Keeper said we should stand at least ten feet away when we pull the ropes. I reckon that'll be your job, Ben, until the girls are older."

At last they were standing at the bottom of a flight of steps leading up to the door of the granite house. "Well, Thankful, what do you think of your new home?"

"I declare, Sam, it's larger than I figured."

They went up the steps with the girls at their heels. The back door opened into a large entry that led directly into a spacious kitchen. Mr. Burgess snatched off his cap, tossed it onto a wooden peg near the doorway, and exclaimed, "We're home!"

Abbie liked their new kitchen immediately. She admired the black stove for it was larger than the one they'd used in

Rockland, and the tank on the back of it would hold more hot water.

The former keeper, who'd sailed from the Rock that morning, had left a fire smoldering inside the stove and a pot of beans simmering on top. At the sink, Abbie pumped water to make coffee for her father and Benjy, and some weak tea and milk for her mother and sisters. She found a storeroom just behind the kitchen, ample for all their rations.

While the girls wandered about peeking around corners, the men hauled a couch from the parlor into the kitchen.

"You rest now, Thankful," Mr. Burgess insisted. "We'll tend to everything." He turned to Benjy. "Build a fire in the fireplace, Son. I'll poke around and see what needs to be done right away. We've got a couple of hours before sunset."

He found a note tacked on the back of the kitchen door. It was a list of instructions and an inventory of supplies. "That's what I call real neighborly," he declared.

While the kettle was heating, Abbie strolled into the parlor. It was furnished with two chairs, a table, settee, and a blanket chest. The plaster walls had been brightened with fresh paint.

She skipped up the stairs to the second floor where her sisters were romping about in the large bedroom which was to be theirs. Abbie was to have the smaller bedroom. Benjy had been assigned a small room behind the storeroom.

There were large oak chiffoniers in both bedrooms, and beds with thin ropes crisscrossed to support the mattresses. A dry sink with a flowered pitcher and matching bowl stood in the far corner of each room. Betty lamps hung on the walls.

Lydia greeted her with, "This room is so full of light,

Abbie! Why, I'll be able to draw even in the wintertime in here."

Esther was leaning on one of the wide window sills, staring out at the water. "Mahala, we could sit up here and play with our dolls. Come look at the gulls—and the ocean."

Abbie followed Mahala to the nearest window, to see what fascinated Esther so. And what a view it was! The Rock was completely encircled by a white-crested ocean that rippled out to the horizon. Gulls darted and dipped, and far out in the distance she saw white specks that must be sails. It was a sight that took her breath away.

Downstairs again, she described the bedrooms to her mother. "The large one is big enough for me and the girls, Mother. And the other one would be just right for you and Father. Won't you change your mind and take it for your room?"

Mrs. Burgess shook her head. "No, Abigail. Climbing those stairs would tucker me out. Your father can fix up that little chamber behind the tower for us. There's plenty of space in the sheds for all the gear that's kept in there now. And the door leads right into the tower, so it's like being part of the main house."

After they all had a brief rest, Benjy carried in the bedding they'd brought. Abbie followed him upstairs to sort it out, so that she and her sisters could make their beds. She was tired from the long trip, and the little ones were irritable, but things had to be settled for the night.

While the girls were struggling with bedsheets and blankets, Abbie filled the chest in the parlor with the rest of their linens. By then, Mr. Burgess and Benjy had rolled in one of the barrels. Benjy began to unpack it.

"Here are the things you'll need for fixing supper, Sis. And cook plenty. I'm starving."

As the girls set the table for supper, they complained of hunger, too. Abbie sliced the leftover bread and cheese. She fried some salt pork to go with the beans on the stove. In the storeroom she found crabapple preserves and a jar of pickles.

Everyone was ravenous when they sat down at the large pine table for their first supper on Matinicus Rock. Mr. Burgess offered a special prayer of thanks for their safe journey from the mainland.

"Bedtime will be early tonight," he said, smiling at the little girls. "Son, after you stow away that pile of beans, we'll go light the lamps."

Abbie's thoughts followed Benjy and her father as they left the kitchen and went into the tower. She was so full of curiosity that she determined to explore the towers tomorrow and see things for herself.

The girls got ready for bed, but they refused to sleep until they'd seen the lighted towers.

When he returned to the kitchen, their father agreed. "The towers are a sight to see. Just wrap up warmly when you come out."

When they were bundled in their wraps, Abbie took one of the small oil lanterns and lighted the way down the steps. It was a calm evening with little wind. There were no gulls about now, and the waves lapped softly at the ledges with a peaceful, murmuring sound.

"Oh!" Lydia exclaimed, as they stared up at the towers. "They're just like jewels shining against the dark sky!"

Mahala clutched Abbie's skirt. "I'm afraid. The lights might fall down on me!"

"Why, Mahala, they won't fall!"

"But they're like big eyes staring down."

Esther and Mahala huddled against her, and Lydia moved closer. Abbie embraced them all. "You shouldn't be frightened by the lights. They're our friends. They're beaming far out into the darkness, warning sailors and ships to beware of running into the Rock. That's why being a lighthouse keeper is a solemn duty. You're beholden to keep the lights burning."

Esther looked up at her. "Will some of the sailors who see the lights come and visit us?"

Abbie laughed. "Not likely. But in the daytime, boats will pass and seamen may wave to us."

Mahala tugged at Abbie's sleeve. "If the light keeps the sailors from wrecking their boats, how can you meet any shipwrecked sailors, the way Benjy allowed?"

"Oh, Mahala, you know Benjy was only fooling. Come, girls, let's go back inside. It's time for bed."

Abbie was exhausted from the long day, but she'd never felt so content. Living on an island, tending a lighthouse, was a great change, but Abbie already felt at home.

CHAPTER V

First Day on the Rock

ABBIE AWOKE the following morning to the smell of frying fish. She washed, dressed, and hurried downstairs. Her father was standing at the stove, turning over thick pieces of fish that were browning in the iron spider.

"Good morning, Daughter," he greeted her. "We're having flounder and potatoes for breakfast."

Abbie smiled sleepily. "Where did the fish come from?"

"I got Benjy up early to help me clean the lamps, so he figured he'd drop a line over the ledge to see what he could outsmart."

"You should have awakened me, Father," Abbie said. "I could have fixed breakfast."

"Well, you can peel those potatoes for me now. Nothing like a good meal to get a day started."

Benjy was across the room, hanging over the fireplace the sword from a swordfish he'd caught on one of his fishing trips. He was proud of his scrimshaw collection, and this was his favorite piece.

"It'll look handsome there, Benjy," Abbie said, as she tied an apron around her dress. "After all the hours you worked carving on it, it deserves a place of honor." She sat down at the table and began peeling the potatoes.

"Benjy and I are obliged to check over provisions today," her father announced, "and we'll have to start on repairs. The water barrels need cleaning."

Finally satisfied with the way the sword looked above the fireplace, Benjy joined Abbie at the table and helped her slice the potatoes. "There's some good fishing out there, Abbie. You should try it sometime."

"I'll leave the fishing to you. Tell me about the lamps. Are they hard to tend?"

Her father spoke first. "For me, the hardest part is climbing stairs in two towers. I reckon I'm not as spry as I once was."

"The stairs are easy," Benjy declared. "It's the smell of that burning whale oil that sickens me."

Mr. Burgess chuckled. "And he doesn't mind the smell of dead fish! I'll take the whale oil any day."

Abbie had imagined that tending the lamps day after day could be monotonous, just as housework sometimes was. But knowing how important the lamps were was bound to ease the work. She was sure that if the lights were her duty, she'd never mind the smell—or the stairs.

After a while, the others joined them for breakfast. They bowed their heads and clasped hands in a circle around the table while Mr. Burgess asked a blessing. "May the Lord preserve thy going out and thy coming in from this time forth and forever more. Amen."

Mrs. Burgess smiled as she looked over the food. "What a fine breakfast, Sam."

"We haven't had fish for breakfast in years and years," Esther observed.

"We haven't done a *lot* of things we'll be doing now," Lydia reminded them. "I like it here, for there's a lot of beautiful scenery, but it's dreadful lonely."

"That's because it's so far out," Benjy said. "It'd take nearly a day to sail to the mainland just to swaps tales a little."

Mr. Burgess stirred sugar into his cup of coffee. "It won't seem lonely after you've been here a while. The supply boat will come every month, and we'll have visitors—whenever the weather's good. Meanwhile, you children are obliged to rely on each other for company. Seems to me that living on a lighthouse station would bring a family closer together."

"Sam, we will have warning when a storm is on the way, won't we?" Mrs. Burgess asked. "I wouldn't worry so, if I knew for sure we'd be prepared."

Mr. Burgess patted his wife's hand. "Thankful, I've been assured that Matinicus Rock is no more dangerous to live on than any other island along the Maine coast. We have a dependable barometer, and Ben and I both have a good weather eye."

Mrs. Burgess smiled wanly. "I suppose I'll always have a fear of the ocean, no matter how beautiful it is."

"You should like the ocean, Mother," Esther said. "Father told us it's our friend because it holds boats up so they can sail on it, and——"

"And it's where the fishes live," Mahala finished.

Abbie had grown troubled as she listened to the others. Suddenly, she blurted, "I don't think it's lonely here. And it's never quiet. Don't you notice the wind and the waves? Why, the Rock's alive with activity—it's like a symphony of the sea."

The others were staring at her in a strange way.

"You're a poet, Sis," Benjy said. "The way you fancy up ordinary things."

After breakfast, Abbie set her sisters to unpacking the contents of the barrels and boxes that had been left overnight in the sheds. Esther stacked the jars of preserves in the storeroom; Lydia placed the ironstone dishes on the shelves of the sideboard in the kitchen; and Mahala arranged the napkins and rings neatly in the drawers below.

While the girls worked, Abbie chopped up the leftover flounder, diced some potatoes and onions, and put it all on to cook. They'd have chowder for dinner. She covered some dried apples with water, to stew later for applesauce.

She helped her mother unroll her treasured braided rug—the one she'd made when a bride—and lay it on the parlor floor. Samplers she'd embroidered were hung on the walls. Pieces of copper the Burgesses had collected, and which Lydia enjoyed polishing, were distributed about until the room had a comfortable, welcoming look.

On top of the blanket chest in the parlor, Abbie lined up her mother's favorite books, including her leather-bound set of the works of Shakespeare, and supported them with the heavy bronze bookends.

During the unpacking, she came across the soap stones. Back in Rockland, she and her sisters often heated them on the stove at night and used them for foot warmers in bed. As she set them on the kitchen hearth, she remembered the wintry nights on which she and Prissy and their friends had taken soap stones along on sleigh rides. Laid beneath their feet, the stones had kept them comfortable for hours as they glided along over the snow. Thinking of Prissy now, she could hardly wait for her to visit the Rock. There was so much to show her!

It was an overcast day, but the wind had lost some of its sting, so it seemed quite balmy to the girls after the long winter. They persuaded Abbie to take them on an outing—a tour of the Rock.

"The *whole* Rock," Mahala insisted. "I want to see that funny-looking fog bell. Father, may I ring it?"

Mr. Burgess chuckled. "I reckon you can try, little one. That reminds me," he continued, "the former Keeper told me that Matinicus Rock is the third foggiest station in Maine. Over seventeen-hundred hours of fog every year. It'll take all of us to keep that bell ringing."

He looked at his wife. "Thankful, I've been meaning to tell you—the girls should wear their hair up in a braid the way you do. It's windy on the Rock most of the year. It may be a lot of trouble to fix, but it would be a heap more trouble to get out the snarls the wind will cause."

"Oh, Mother, may we?" Abbie asked eagerly. Most girls had to wait until they were eighteen or so to put up their hair. "Won't our mainland friends be impressed? I can hardly wait for Prissy to see us."

After the dinner dishes were cleared away, the girls brought their hairbrushes downstairs. Mrs. Burgess sat on the couch and braided Mahala's long blond hair, then wrapped it around her head and fastened it securely with large hairpins. "Now, Abbie, you may try."

It was a struggle to match her mother's skill, but Abbie

persisted until Esther and Lydia also had braids around their heads. Mrs. Burgess then put up Abbie's long hair.

"There now, you can go outside," she said at last. "I have four little women."

Mahala beamed. "That's what *I* am, Mother! Don't you recollect that Father told me my name is the Indian word for 'little woman?' "

Eager for their outing, Mahala and Esther skipped down the steps ahead of Abbie, and Lydia followed with her sketching tablet and charcoal crayon. They walked around to the front of the house, then moved back to get a clearer view of the front of it with its towers situated at each end.

Near the house, the rock surface was smooth, but the farther away from the house they went, the rougher it became. Almost immediately, Mahala stumbled. Abbie picked her up and quieted her whimpering.

"You must watch your step, Mahala. You can't run and skip across rocks."

Lydia, unmindful of the episode, announced, "I've decided to sketch the house first. It's so handsome. But I wish we had some trees around here."

Abbie strolled over to the sheds, opened the doors, and peered inside. Another dory, smaller than the *Provider,* was stored in the boathouse. The other sheds were crowded with shelves covered with paint pots, tools, and heavy rope coiled neatly in the corners.

Lydia tugged her arm. "It's just old fishing gear, Abbie. Let's sit a spell so I can sketch some."

"Very well," Abbie agreed. She turned to take Mahala's hand, but only Esther stood there. "Where's Mahala?" Abbie asked.

"She went over that way." Esther pointed toward the back of the house.

Abbie hurried in that direction, with Lydia and Esther following. Around the side of the house, they came upon their father and Benjy scraping on the inside of a huge rain barrel that had been removed from the back of the house. Mahala poked her head out of the center of the barrel.

"Look, Abbie—it's just like the rain barrel we had at the other house. Father says he'll put charcoal in it, too—to keep the water clean."

Mr. Burgess glanced up, frowning. "You'd better keep Mahala from underfoot, Abigail. Take the girls down to that little cove and let them watch the birds."

Mahala and Esther dashed ahead, anxious to see the birds. They'd gone only a few yards when they tripped and sprawled on the rocks.

"Sakes' alive!" Abbie lifted them both up. After that, the little ones stepped over the rocky surface with great care.

Near the cove, the Rock sloped down to the water, then dropped abruptly. Abbie held out her hands to keep the girls back until she was sure it was safe to continue. Afterward she let them crawl on their hands and knees and peer over the ledge.

Lydia stared, her eyes wide with awe. "There are dozens of birds down below."

"Look at those funny-looking Rock birds!" Esther cried.

"I'll sketch those first," Lydia declared. "They're fancier than just plain old gulls."

There was a crying sound behind them, like the wail of a baby. The girls hushed their chatter and looked around. Seeing only sea gulls, they laughed together. All of a sudden, several gulls flapped their wings and darted higher into the air. Seconds later, there was a crashing sound, and the gulls dove down toward the Rock.

"Did you see that?" Lydia whispered. "Those gulls dropped some mussels on the ground, and now they're eating them."

"Gulls are quite intelligent," Abbie told them. "They've learned they must break the shells open to get to the meat inside."

"There goes another one!" Esther shrieked, as a gull swirled directly over her head.

"Look behind you, Esther," Lydia said in a low voice, "There's one coming toward us." A slick gray-and-white gull stood scarcely ten feet away, its head cocked. After staring at them with one eye, the gull turned its head to the other side, and stared out of the other eye.

Lydia had a look of surprise. "Why, they have *orange* eyes!" She leaned back slowly, pulling her sketching tablet toward her. "I'm going to draw him," she said. But when she sat up, the gull flew away.

While they were watching the sunlight play on the tumbling waves, a small black hump rolled over in the water near the edge of the reef.

"That's a seal!" Mahala jumped up and down. "Will it climb up here, Abbie?"

"Not likely. It's probably frightened of us."

Mahala sat down beside Abbie. "Would Father let us keep it for a pet?"

"Be your age, Mahala," Lydia said. "You know seals can't live out of water."

"But he could live in the ocean and still be our pet—couldn't he?"

Abbie smoothed Mahala's hair. "Of course, he could. What shall we name him?"

"Let's call him Sammy—after Father."

Abbie protested, but Mahala and Esther had their minds set on that name.

"We've got to go now," Abbie told them presently. "I can't leave you down here alone." As they neared the house, she stopped in front of the first tower and looked upward.

"Are we going inside?" Mahala asked. "Can we light the lamps?"

"Don't ever bother those lamps, Mahala. That's Father's job—and Benjy's. I just want to go up the stairs and see the lamp room." She opened the wooden door, and her sisters went in ahead of her. As the door shut, a rush of air passed through the tall shaft.

The base of the tower appeared to be a storage place for barrels, oil cans, and coils of rope, all properly stacked.

Abbie went over to the narrow stairway with its handrail made of thick rope that spiraled up to the top of the tower. She glanced back at her sisters. "My heart's set on it, Lydia. I'll think of nothing else until I see those lamps."

"Not me," Lydia retorted. "It's dark and ugly in here."

Mahala was swinging on the railing. "I want to ring the fog bell."

"And I'm hungry," Esther whined.

Abbie let out a sigh. "You'd best take them back to the house, Lydia. You can go through the inside door. I won't be long."

Once they were gone, she began to climb. She stepped

lightly, yet the sound of her footsteps boomed in the granite tower. Ten, eleven, twelve, she counted. She came to a landing where light shone through a small window just above. She stopped briefly to catch her breath, then went on, counting aloud.

Forty-five, forty-six, forty-seven, forty-eight. . . . She stepped into the lamp room with her heart pounding fiercely. The first thing she noticed was a peculiar odor. Then she saw the circular shelf where the Argand lamps, unlighted now, were arranged in a horizontal row. Next, her eyes were drawn up to the window, and the view from it held her spellbound. Gray water, billowing into waves, stretched on endlessly. The waves moved in such a way that the tower itself seemed to be flowing along with them.

The lamp room formed a world completely apart from the Rock below, from the world she'd left. Her mind turned over the words that had passed at dinner. Lydia and Benjy thought of the Rock as lonely, and her mother was frightened of the ocean. But Abbie was overjoyed to know that this was her world now, to live in and to love.

Abbie Burgess, the gulls seemed to be shouting to her, welcome to Matinicus Rock!

CHAPTER VI

A Week Passes

ABBIE LAID ASIDE the volume of Whittier's poems she'd been reading, and turned her attention to the arithmetic problems her father had written on her slate.

It was their third evening on the Rock, and her parents had decided it was high time the children settled down to their schoolwork. Hornbooks, almanacs, geography, and arithmetic books had been unpacked and brought to the kitchen for study. An oil lamp burned in the center of the pine table.

While Esther and Mahala were reciting aloud from Mc-Guffey's Reader, Lydia struggled over an essay she'd been assigned to write. Even Benjy did not escape his parents' demands. If he was set on taking his place in the world, he'd be obliged, his father told him, to know how to figure sums and balance books. So now he was poring over two pages of problems involving barrels of fish, pounds of twine, and miles of ocean.

After arithmetic lessons, and a recitation period, Mr. Burgess went on to their geography lesson. He unfolded a map and spread it out on the table.

"I found this in the lighthouse—appears to be handmade. It's a pen-and-ink drawing of the Maine coast, dotted with hundreds of islands."

The children leaned over the table and studied the map, while their father pointed out Matinicus Rock and drew the route they had sailed from the mainland. He talked about high and low tides, and described various types of storms, such as gales, sou'westers, nor'easters, and blizzards.

Abbie couldn't fathom why her father brought up the subject that distressed her mother so, but she understood as he continued, "In my lifetime, I've weathered nearly every kind of storm there is, and I'm still here to tell of it. The trick is to know how to protect yourself and your craft, how to handle a boat, keep it afloat. You girls aren't too young to start learning such things. And it's important to have a weather eye.

"There's an old sailor's poem that helps many a fisherman. 'When the wind is to the North, the fisherman he goes not forth. When the wind is to the East, 'tis neither good for man nor beast. When the wind is to the South, it blows the bait in the fishes' mouth. When the wind is to the West, then 'tis at the very best.' "

"My favorite," Abbie spoke up, "is 'Red at night, sailor's delight. Red at dawning, sailors take warning.' That one's taken from the Bible—in Matthew," she added proudly.

" 'Rain before seven, clear before eleven,' " Benjy volunteered. " 'And a sunshiny shower won't last half an hour.' "

"I know one," Esther blurted. " 'Fishy, fishy, come bite my hook. I'll go captain, and you'll go cook.' "

"That's not a seaman's weather poem," Lydia chided her. "It's just a nursery rhyme."

Mahala touched the edge of the map. "Is this the end of the world, Father—right here?"

Mr. Burgess laughed merrily. "That seems a logical question, little one," he replied. "I reckon we need a lot more lessons in geography."

"Father," Abbie inquired now, "the girls and I are curious about the Rock birds, where they come from——"

"I asked the former Keeper about them, Daughter. He said they live near the Arctic. When it grows cold there, they fly South—and nest here on the Rock where it's warmer. Sounds strange to say it's warmer here, but it is, compared to the Arctic."

Mrs. Burgess began stacking the books. "It's late, Sam. Time the children went to bed. Lydia, read your piece for us."

Lydia cleared her throat, and began, "Living on a lighthouse is interesting. If you like such things, there are towers to light, and a house to clean, and fish to fish out of the ocean. If you're an artist as I am—oh, well, at least there are some interesting things to paint . . ."

When she finished, her mother said, "That's fine, Lydia."

Mr. Burgess looked over Benjy's arithmetic paper. "Son, your business would fail in no time if this is how you calculate."

"But I'd be keener about figures, if I were on my own."

"That may be, but I won't accept slipshod work." He made corrections, turned the paper over, and handed it back. "Now, figure again."

Benjy worked over the problems grimly. Finally, he gave

the paper back and got to his feet. "Want me to check the lamps, Father?"

Mr. Burgess nodded. "Take Abbie with you—show her what the towers are like at night."

Benjy lighted a lantern and led the way from the kitchen into the tower. Abbie followed eagerly, lifting her long dress so she could move more quickly.

"This work isn't nearly as hard as Father allows," Benjy said as they were mounting the spiral stairway. "All it takes is a strong back, and a poor sense of smell."

Benjy had no sooner spoken than Abbie discovered what he meant. Drawing near the lamp room, she detected the same peculiar odor she'd noticed before, only it was stronger now.

"Sakes' alive!" she gasped, falling back against the rope railing. The lard oil that burned in their Betty lamps and lanterns had a certain odor about it, but it was mild compared to burning whale oil.

Benjy chuckled. "Want to swap chores with me now?"

She sat down on the steps. "I'll just sit a spell until I get used to it."

When they entered the lamp room a few minutes later, the light from the lamps was so brilliant and white that it made her eyes smart. As she paused there, she was thrilled to think that these very lamps, shining out beyond the barren reefs, beyond the Rock, might be keeping some ship from running aground.

"Come, Sis," Benjy urged. "We've got to check the other tower."

They walked down the steps, through the inside door into the house, then through the parlor and into the second tower. This time, Abbie braced herself. Burning whale oil was a far cry from the fresh salt air that blew across the Rock, but she supposed unpleasant things had to be endured for the sake of a worthy purpose.

When they returned to the kitchen, the others were sitting about the table. Mr. Burgess looked up from the large family Bible opened in front of him.

"We're still in Proverbs," he began, as Benjy and Abbie took their places. The family smiled as his voice boomed out, " 'The name of the Lord is a strong tower: The righteous runneth into it, and is safe.' "

Friday turned out to be the busiest day of the week. At breakfast, Mr. Burgess assigned chores. Mahala, Esther, and Lydia groaned when he told them they were to begin polishing the brass in the towers—oil cans, dust pans, and doorknobs.

Benjy's job, after he ran the flag up the pole, was to stir up a pot of whitewash and apply a fresh coat of it on the north tower.

"Keeping the dwellings shipshape is part of the job here," their father explained. "A government inspector comes out every few months, and we can't afford to have him turn in a bad report on us."

"An inspector?" Abbie was concerned. "When will he visit us?"

"We won't know, Daughter, until we sight him offshore. But don't fret. The Lighthouse Board doesn't expect a keeper to do much repairing until spring. After Ben and I finish the barrels, we'll paint the dory. And we'll be making some buoys for lobstering—out of those logs that drifted up on the shore. You girls can paint them for us. Thankful, I'm counting on you to keep a list of supplies we'll need to pick up when we go into Rockland."

Before the girls began their outside work, they had to tend to their household chores. The little ones swept and dusted; Lydia filled the pitchers in the bedrooms with fresh water; all of them made their beds and helped Abbie with the dishes.

After dinner, while the others were outside, and her mother was napping, Abbie got busy scrubbing the kitchen floor. Down on her knees in the quiet house, she thought back over the days since their arrival. There'd been a lot of talk about how lonely and far out they were, but each day they fussed a little less. Even her mother complained very little about her ailments, or the noise the ocean made. Abbie was sure they were bound to like it here, for there were so many challenging things to do.

Saturday began pleasantly, with everyone attending to chores. The girls polished brass, and Benjy helped his father replace the rain barrels against the house.

Not long after dinner, Abbie heard her brother shouting outside. She ran to the door, her heart pounding in alarm. He was pointing toward the sea. "There's a school of herring swimming by!"

She dashed down the steps and followed Benjy to the shed where their father was working. As she reached the doorway, she heard him say, "Hoist a bushel basket up on the flagpole, Son—quick. That's the signal the keepers use to tell the fishermen."

Abbie stepped inside. "But the fish will be gone before anyone can row over here."

Benjy grinned. "Don't fret, Sis. It takes hours for a school of fish to pass the Rock." He unraveled some fishing nets. "How about some fresh herring for supper?"

The girls stopped their work and came down to the landing to watch while Benjy put the small fishing boat out on the water. Esther and Mahala made a game out of counting the silvery herring as they flashed through the waves.

Lydia smiled over at Abbie. "Benjy's happy as a clam at high tide."

Abbie nodded thoughtfully. "The sea's in his blood, Lydia. Fishing means as much to him as drawing does to you."

"I wish Father understood that. Abbie, couldn't you talk him into letting me help paint the dory? That way, I'd be painting instead of polishing brass."

"I'll see what I can do," she promised.

Hours of physical labor and the fresh sea air had created enormous appetites, but potatoes, vegetables, pie—and the fresh herring Benjy had caught and Abbie fried—quickly satisfied all.

After Benjy and his father left to light the lamps, Abbie and Lydia brought the wooden tub out of the storeroom and put it on the floor close to the warm stove. The water tank on the back of the stove had been heating since afternoon, so there was plenty to fill the tub.

On each side of the tub, Abbie placed a chair to hold night clothes and bath towels. Mahala and Esther undressed and climbed into the tub, giggling all the while. After they lathered themselves well, Abbie rinsed them with warm water poured from the kettle.

Ready for bed, the two younger girls went to their mother's room where she read to them while the older girls took over the kitchen. After their baths were over, Lydia and Abbie joined the others for the nightly hairbrushing ritual. Standing close in a circle, each sister brushed the long hair of the one in front of her, all counting in unison. When they'd finished one hundred strokes, they flopped on their mother's bed to rest, begging her to tell another tale of her girlhood in Maine.

On Sunday morning, Benjy asked his father when he planned to sail back to the mainland for the rest of their belongings.

"I've been studying on it, Son, but I can't figure how both of us could go. Even with a good wind, it'll take a whole day to make the round trip. One of us is obliged to stay to light the lamps at sunset."

Benjy brightened. "I'd be pleasured to make the trip alone, Father. I can handle the dory. I'll ask Mr. Pratt to lend me a wagon, and Fred can help me load everything into the boat."

Mrs. Burgess was shaking her head. "Mercy, Sam, you daren't let Benjy make that trip alone! He's just a boy!"

"He's nearly seventeen, Thankful, with as much growth as a man. He can do the job as well as I can." He turned to Abbie. "I don't hold to letting a young girl do man's work, but it's best that you learn the ropes, Daughter—for just such times as this. Some keepers teach their entire families how to operate the lamps."

"Father," Lydia cried, "please don't make me work around those smelly old lamps! I couldn't bear it!"

"I'll help you, Father," Abbie said. "Lydia can take over some of my chores whenever I tend the lamps."

"Very well, then." Mr. Burgess turned to Benjy. "You should leave for Rockland at dawn tomorrow, so get the dory ready this afternoon."

The girls bustled about putting the parlor in order for the family's Sunday meeting. Now that they were unable to attend church in Rockland, Mr. Burgess planned to conduct a family service here on the Rock.

Mrs. Burgess made herself comfortable on the settee, and the little ones snuggled against her. Abbie and Lydia took the straight chairs, and Benjy straddled the footstool.

One of the small tables had been moved in front of the window, and Mr. Burgess stood on one side of it, rubbing his beard.

"Esther, you're the songbird of the family. How about leading us in 'Rock of Ages'?"

They all joined in singing the words they had come to cherish. One hymn followed another, and finally Mr. Burgess began the sermon.

"I'll read the story of Elijah, who called upon God to burn the wood which the worshipers of Baal had failed to do," he said.

Abbie listened earnestly to her father expound the text, calling their attention to Elijah's deep faith. He likened their giving up their home in Rockland for a new life here on the Rock to Elijah's experience, for their move was surely a challenge to their faith in God's protection.

She always admired the sermons her father added to the nightly Bible readings, but today's sermon impressed Abbie even more. His long, inspired prayer that followed prompted her to wish she could pray as eloquently. Since women were never called upon to pray in public, it was unlikely that she would ever do so. Only men, it seemed to her, were allowed to do the *interesting* things in life, such as keeping light-houses and sailing ships.

The prospect of taking Benjy's place beside her father for even one day lifted her spirits no end. She could hardly wait to do it and later to tell Prissy about it.

CHAPTER VII

Abbie Helps Tend the Lamps

ABBIE'S FATHER woke her before dawn the next morning. "I'll get the fire going and help Ben lower the dory," he said. "You get some breakfast for us."

The fire in the stove was roaring away when Abbie reached the kitchen, and slices of salt pork were browning in the spider. She pumped water at the sink, filled the coffee pot, and put it on the stove. She mixed up dough, and dropped out biscuits, making a few extra for Benjy's lunch. She cut the balance of the apple pie into two generous slices and set them on the table.

While the biscuits were baking, she stepped outside to see what kind of weather Benjy would have for sailing. A fresh, mild wind fanned her cheeks. She breathed deeply until she felt her lungs would burst. She was sure she'd never be able to live anywhere else again except on the Rock. Yet, her father might not be reappointed. She shook her head, as if to rid herself of such a dreadful thought. It was silly to spoil this glorious day speculating about the future.

After breakfast, with the lunch basket on her arm, she strolled down to the landing with Benjy. Their father walked ahead, swinging a lantern.

The glow from the lighted towers was shining out, illuminating the landing site. Abbie waited above on the ledge while the two men slid the dory down the ways and out on the water. As the boat bobbed about on the waves, its sail bending in the gentle wind, she called, "Take care, Benjy!"

Mr. Burgess trudged back up the stone steps, holding the lantern high. "The sea's calm today. He'll have a nice sail. Now, Daughter, we'll tend to those lamps."

Going into the first tower, he told her, "This is no work for a young girl, but next to Ben, you're the only one I can rightly count on."

"I understand, Father. Really, I don't mind."

He went about his work, blowing out the lamps, one by one. After the glass chimneys were cool, he removed them and put them aside. "Now, we've got to clean the lamp bowls, trim the wicks, and refill them with oil. I'll show you how it's done, and then let you try a few."

Working alongside her father, Abbie wiped the bowls with one of the rags kept on hand for just that purpose. Once the lamps were finished, they polished the silvered reflectors. Their work done in the first tower, they walked back down the stairs, through the house, and up the stairs of the second tower, where they went through the same procedure.

Feeling properly awed over being an assistant Keeper for a day, Abbie returned to the kitchen and served breakfast to the others.

Ordinarily, Monday would have been washday, but because of Abbie's extra duties, Mrs. Burgess changed it to baking day. Abbie helped her mother mix up a large bowl of dough, knead it, and shape it into loaves that, when baked, would be their bread supply for the coming week.

Meanwhile, her father set up shop on a level spot at the rear of the house. With wooden slats, tools, and a keg of nails piled around him, he began to build the needed lobster traps.

After their noonday meal, Abbie went outside to see how his work was progressing. The girls were helping him: Esther was stacking wooden slats according to length; Mahala was handing nails to her father; and Lydia was sitting on the bottom step, tying twine into small squares with a wooden tool she called a needle.

"Lydia caught on quick to knitting those 'heads,' " her father said, looking pleased.

Lydia sighed. "I'd rather polish doorknobs."

"Now, child, I can't do without those heads. When the lobster crawls inside the trap after the bait, his claws get snarled up in the knitted head, and he can't escape."

"What will you use for bait?" Abbie asked.

"Rotten fish, well salted."

Lydia gasped. "How horrid!"

Mr. Burgess chuckled. "You won't notice it long's the wind's in the other direction. Hand me another slat, Esther."

Her father's plans for lobstering reminded Abbie of Benjy's yearning to leave. "How many traps will you need to start?"

"About forty. We can work those during the day, and make more traps in the evening. I'm aiming for an even hundred."

"But if Benjy weren't here to help you—could you still handle a hundred traps?"

He stroked his beard. "Aye, if I pulled half one day, and half another." He shrugged. "If Ben decided to leave, I reckon I'd have to work half as many traps as I figured. But he'll like it here, once we put out in the boat every day."

Abbie went back inside the house and said to her mother, "It's such a beautiful day, why don't you come outside for a spell? Bring your afghan. I'll haul your rocker out there, and you don't have to worry about the bread—I'll put it in the oven now and keep an eye on it."

She situated her mother in a comfortable spot near the outdoor workshop. Mahala and Esther skipped about, showing her the task each one had been assigned.

"Hand me that needle," Mrs. Burgess said to Lydia, "I've a mind to try my hand at one of those heads."

The pungent aroma of the baking yeast bread soon reached Abbie's nostrils. She dashed up the steps and into the kitchen. The loaves were perfect; plump and golden brown, the way Benjy fancied them. But she mustn't think of Benjy so much. After today, he'd probably sail to Rockland as often as he could. Before long, he would surely leave for good.

When she went back outside, she missed Mahala.

"The last I saw of her," Lydia offered, "she was playing with rocks over by that tower."

Lydia had hardly spoken the words when Mahala shouted at them, "Look at me! Look at me!" She was up on the catwalk at the top of the north tower, leaning against the railing.

Mr. Burgess dropped his hammer and hustled toward the tower. Mrs. Burgess covered her face with her hands, moaning, "That child, that child!"

Abbie's first instinct was to follow her father, but her

mother needed her more. "Don't be afraid, Mother. Father will have her down in no time."

Esther and Lydia stood below the tower, yelling up to their little sister. "Go back inside, Mahala—*please!*"

To everyone's relief, Mr. Burgess soon had Mahala in tow. When he brought her back to the group, she was beaming proudly. "Did you see me, Mother—up high?"

"You frightened us out of our wits, child," Mrs. Burgess scolded as she clung to her youngest. "How could you do such a foolish thing?"

Mahala hugged her mother. "I had a mind to climb the steps."

"You were just trying to get attention," Lydia declared. "You're *always* getting attention."

Mr. Burgess took Mahala's hand and led her up the steps. "No more sashaying around for you today. You'll stay in your room until supper."

After the two had disappeared into the house, Esther began to whimper. "I don't want Father to punish Mahala, even if she is naughty."

"She deserves it," Lydia snapped, tying heads again.

Mrs. Burgess wiped her eyes. "Abigail, don't you see how dangerous life is here? The tower, the rocks, the ocean—sometimes I'm nearly afraid to breathe."

"Oh, Mother, Mahala's bound to get into trouble, no matter where we live. She's curious and high spirited. If there weren't any dangers around, she'd surely invent some."

Presently, Mr. Burgess returned. "We're obliged to keep a close haul on that child. I spanked her, but she'll still be getting into mischief."

"Sam," Mrs. Burgess fretted, "we shouldn't have come here—not with these little ones."

"Now, Thankful, other keepers raised children on the Rock. Some were even a bit younger than ours. Their wanderings were cured by putting them on ropes."

"*Ropes?* Oh, Sam!"

"It isn't near as cruel as it sounds. We'll tie a rope harness on Mahala with enough length to allow her some freedom, without going beyond the point of safety. It'll protect her, and give us some peace."

Abbie wasn't sure she could bear to see Mahala's vitality thwarted by a rope, but there seemed to be no other way. It was getting late, so she carried the rocker back inside. Her mother followed and lay down on the couch.

"I was feeling so much better," she said. "Then Mahala scared the strength right out of me."

"We were all shaken, Mother. You just lie there and rest while I fix the food."

"Mercy, Abigail. I may not be strong, but I'm no invalid. Let's have a boiled supper tonight. I'll peel the potatoes and you can do the onions. We'll use up that salt beef we brought with us."

While Abbie was setting the table, she passed the kitchen window. She stopped still, hoping her eyes were playing tricks on her. She knew it couldn't be Mahala, for she was up in her room. Yet, only Mahala's hair glistened like gold in the sunlight.

Abbie wasted no time explaining the situation to her mother. "I'll be back soon," she called as she hurried out of the kitchen and through the outside tower door. She ran across the rocks toward the fog bell, her heart thudding.

When she reached Mahala, she grabbed her and stood her on the ground. "How dare you disobey Father and leave your room? How dare you climb up on the bell, when it's forbidden? Now you'll really be punished!"

Mahala wrestled free and darted away. "Let's go see the birds now!"

Lightning quick, Abbie caught the skirt of Mahala's long dress. "No, we're not going down there. You've been a naughty girl today."

With a firm hand on her sister's arm, Abbie led her along to the house. "Mahala, it's high time you realized how much you upset everyone when you do these things. And no matter how you fancy the birds, you daren't go down there alone. And don't ever, ever try to climb over the side of the Rock. You might slip and fall, and we wouldn't be able to hear you call for help with the waves pounding so hard."

Mahala began to whimper, and by the time her father had finished admonishing her, she was sobbing. "Up to your room until study time!" he ordered. "You'll have supper in your room!"

Abbie served supper early so that she could help her father light the lamps before sunset. Despite the good food and delicious fresh bread, they ate in awkward silence.

Esther finally spoke up. "Father, may I take some supper up to Mahala now? She's so little."

Her father nodded. "Aye. You may take it to her, Esther." At these words, everyone cheered up.

Leaving Lydia and Esther to clear away the dishes, Abbie climbed the tower steps behind her father, who carried a lantern to brighten their way.

In the lamp room, he removed the glass chimneys from the

lamps, then lit a candle and held it to each wick until it flamed up. He put each glass chimney securely in place before he went on to the next lamp.

"Tending these lamps is a heap easier in spring and summer, Daughter. Come winter, there'll be ice and snow to scrape off the outside of the windows. Always keep in mind— these lamps are the most important thing on the Rock. The fog bell has its purpose, but the lamps in these towers must never be allowed to go out—from sunset to sunrise."

Abbie swallowed hard, thinking what a challenge that would be.

When her father had the last lamp glowing, Abbie said quietly, "Now Benjy will have a light to guide him into the cove."

Her father patted her hand. "He'll be along in time. Benjy's a good seaman."

She had no doubts about her brother's seamanship, but still she wondered about him. Her mother imagined all sorts of dreadful things befalling Benjy out at sea, but Abbie worried about his comfort. Was he cold? Was he drenched from the sea? Would his food supply last? She'd looked after the family's needs for so long that she could not rest easy when a loved one was away from home.

She returned to the kitchen, where she found her sisters engrossed in their studies.

"Father's gone down to the landing to see if he can sight Benjy offshore," Abbie told her mother.

"That boy should have been back before now. I can't stop fretting when he's out on the water at night."

Abbie reassured her mother that all was well, but she herself listened intently for footsteps. After a time, there was a shuffling sound outside. The door burst open, and Mr. Burgess trudged in, followed by Benjy, who looked quite weary, though he had a smile for all.

Lydia flung her arms around him, and the younger girls jumped about gleefully. "What did you bring us?" they chorused.

Benjy hugged each one. When he got to Abbie, he whirled her around. "I saw Prissy today. She was all rigged out, riding down the street in a fine carriage. She waved at me."

Abbie sat her brother down at the table and served his supper. "We can have a good chowder tomorrow, Sis," he told her. "I brought back some fresh milk. And there's some fruit and those spices you wanted so much." He called off the balance of supplies he'd brought, including a new barometer from headquarters. "Guess they figure Father should have one in each tower."

The girls went through the pockets of his coat, pulled out several packages, and brought them over to the table. "Here are some penny China dolls Mr. Pratt sent to Esther and Mahala," Benjy explained. He handed over a length of lace for Abbie and her mother and a pressed fern for Lydia. "The fern is slightly damaged," he apologized, "but it came all the way from Australia."

Benjy inquired about their day.

"We built lobster traps," Lydia said as she and the younger girls went over to sit by the fire and admire their gifts.

"So you're serious about lobstering," Benjy said to his father.

"Aye. Forty traps will yield a barrel, and at twenty dollars a barrel, I calculate we'll be paid well for our labors. There'll be plenty left for us to relish. Lobster—now there's a dish fit for a king!"

Benjy glanced at Abbie. "How do you like tending the lamps?"

"She caught on quick, Son," Mr. Burgess put in before Abbie could speak. "But we all know Abbie's smart."

"And strong, too," Benjy pointed out. "She could help you same as I could. And Lydia's old enough to be of some use with the lobstering."

Abbie frowned at Benjy, for she knew where his words were leading. Her father sensed it, too. "The women have their work, Son, and we have ours."

His words were firm, but Abbie knew that words wouldn't hold Benjy long. One day soon, he'd leave the Rock.

CHAPTER VIII

⚓

Spring Arrives

"ALL I DO IS WORK," Lydia fumed as she pinned another dress on the clothesline. "I did my chores, picked meat out of those old lobster shells, scrubbed clothes on the washboard, and now I'm hanging them out. Abbie, I'll never draw anything really pretty if I'm obliged to work *all* the time."

Mahala handed Abbie another pair of trousers from the washbasket. Abbie shook them, then fastened them on the line. "You should be glad you're strong enough to work, Lydia. Think of Father and Benjy out there in the dory— would you rather be helping them haul in lobster traps?"

"*I* would!" Mahala exclaimed. "I wish Father would let *me* help."

Esther, who was stooping over the washbasket and handing wash to Lydia, blurted, "You just hanker to jump in that ocean, so you can get some more attention, Mahala. *I'm* the one who should help Father."

Mahala clamped her hands on her hips and flared, "And you'd bring more lobsters home to eat than Father allows!"

Esther narrowed her eyes. "You ate more lobster yesterday than *I* did."

"Girls, girls!" Abbie separated them before they could tussle. "Lydia and I will finish hanging up the wash. You two go inside and help Mother."

After the younger ones were gone, Lydia said, "You see, Abbie? They're tired of working, too. Isn't there something we can do that's fun?" She shook out another garment. "I guess it's spring we miss. There's no grass here to tumble on, no trees to sit under, no jonquils or crocuses to gather. There aren't any berries to pick, and Mother can't even plant a garden. We're just stuck here on this drab old Rock——"

"I miss things, too, Lydia. I miss the flowers and berries and grass. Life is different here, but there's plenty to enjoy. We'll go wading in the tide this afternoon. There was a full moon last night, and Benjy told me that means the tide is higher than usual. The gulls are molting now, too. The girls could gather up their feathers. And the crabs will be wriggling out of their old shells. They outgrow them every spring, you know, and shed them on the shore. We just have to look about for things to do."

She smoothed the hem of one of her mother's dresses as she added, "We don't have trees, but we have a cool breeze. We don't have neighbors, but we've got some glorious scenery. Look out there, Lydia. Those white specks are sailboats—they'll probably pass the Rock after a while."

Sometime later, the kitchen door slammed and Esther skipped down the steps and sat down. "I sampled the lobster stew for you, Abbie. It's delicious."

Abbie smiled. "And what is Mahala up to?"

"She came outside. Didn't you see her?"

"No—— Oh, Esther, she's probably gone to see the birds!
Why didn't you tell me?" Abbie darted around the front of
the house, yelling, "Mahala, where are you?"

There was no sign of her near the tower, the fog bell, nor
the sheds, so Abbie headed for the crevice on the Rock where
the birds nested. But Mahala wasn't there, either. She turned
then and sprinted in the direction of the cove. Her breath cut
sharply into her chest, but she didn't dare stop running until
she'd reached the ledge.

"Mahala," she called down, *"answer me!"*

A little head ducked out from behind a cavelike opening
near the bottom of the Rock. "Look at me, Abbie!"

"Mahala, come out of there! Don't you see the waves dash-
ing against those rocks? Hurry, before you're drenched!"

"I'm all over wet," Mahala announced. She crawled out,
her long skirt clinging to her legs. She groped her way up the
jagged surface to the ledge, where Abbie pulled her up and
stood her on her feet.

"This is a fine kettle of fish, Mahala! Every time I take my
eyes off you, you run away—right into trouble. Don't you see
the tide washing over those rocks? Soon the cave will be filled
with water, and you'd have been trapped there."

Lydia and Esther caught up with them and joined in the
scolding.

"This settles it," Abbie said on the way back to the house.
"Father will put you on a rope now."

She put Mahala in a corner of the parlor, facing the wall.
"If you move from there," she warned, "you won't get one
mouthful of dinner."

The prospect of Mahala spending her hours outdoors in a
rope harness dampened the family's enjoyment of the lobster

stew. But Mahala herself was nonchalant about her fate until she discovered that the rope would not reach as far as she wanted to explore.

Abbie had remained in the kitchen while her father tied Mahala into the harness. Now she wanted to go outside, to explain again to her little sister that they were doing this for her protection. But before she could do so, she overheard Esther talking to Mahala.

"Don't you fret, Sister. I'll play with you. I'll bring all our dolls outside. And Abbie promised to take us wading this afternoon."

Abbie didn't know whether to laugh or cry. This morning, they had been quarreling; now they were the best of friends. Her father was right, Abbie thought. Not having outsiders to lean on did bring a family closer together.

The younger girls played quietly, and Lydia strolled over by the fog bell and settled down with her sketching tablet. Abbie took the dry clothes from the clothesline, sprinkled them, and rolled them into bundles. Tomorrow, while her mother mended torn garments, and Lydia replaced missing buttons, she would iron them.

She had just finished when Lydia burst into the kitchen. "A supply boat's coming! It's heading straight for the Rock! Father and Benjy are on their way to the landing. You should see Mahala," she went on with a chuckle. "She's furious because the rope won't reach that far."

"Stay with the two girls, Lydia," Mrs. Burgess said. "You'll only be in the way if you go down there."

Abbie's heart quickened in anticipation. At last, the supply boat had come! She thought of their rations first, then the mail. Would there be a letter from Prissy? Just when she could bear the suspense no longer, her father entered, laden with packages and newspapers. He handed several letters to Abbie's mother. "And here's one for you, Daughter." His dark eyes twinkled.

The envelope was addressed in Prissy's flowery handwriting. Abbie tore the seal open and unfolded a large sheet of paper. She stared at it. The entire page had been written upon. Prissy had begun in the usual fashion, from left to right, but at the bottom she continued to write up the side, over the top, and around to the bottom again.

"This is the latest fad in Rockland," Prissy stated, "and I'm glad to have the extra space to tell you my news. I've missed you so, Abbie. There's no one to share my secrets with now, and I have so *many* secrets. Isn't there some way you could visit Rockland? I saw Benjy the other day. He looked so manly, swaggering along the waterfront."

Abbie read the letter aloud to her mother, who laughed softly at Prissy's wordy observations. She later went outside to read the letter to Esther and Mahala, but they scarcely listened. She'd expected Lydia, at least, to appreciate Prissy's girlish gossip, but Lydia was enthralled with the envelope of buttons she'd received from Mrs. Haskell, a dressmaker in Rockland, who'd become a family friend.

"Look at this button, Abbie. Mrs. Haskell says it's from a Sunday dress that belonged to the mayor's wife. She's having a new one made. And this one——"

Abbie admired the buttons, but her thoughts were troubled over the distance between the two of them. Though she was only three years younger, Lydia wasn't mature enough to take Prissy's place. But Abbie reasoned with herself that she didn't need a close friend. There was so much to do here, so much that pleasured her more than simple friendship.

Benjy and his father hauled in the quarterly allowance of provisions the supply boat had brought out to them from the mainland. They stood the barrel of flour in the storeroom, set other items on shelves, and hung dried beef and pork on the walls. Abbie surveyed it all contentedly. What grand meals they'd have!

When she spoke of their abundance of rations at supper, Esther brightened, "Father, could we have lobster more than twice a week, now?"

Mr. Burgess laughed. "Lobster on Sundays, and stew on Mondays is plenty for anyone, even my hungry little Esther. But we needn't limit ourselves to lobster. These waters are rich with fish just as tasty. Now that summer's nearly here, you girls can gather the crabs that cluster on the side of the Rock. They'll make a fine stew. Once Benjy and I have a chance to fish more, we'll smoke some and store it for winter. And there's a sea moss," he went on, "strewn along the water's edge that can be used for food. After it's dried out, it can be pulverized into a powder that'll thicken into a pudding right well."

Esther gasped. "A *pudding!* Oh, Father, Mahala and I will gather all the sea moss on the whole Rock!"

Abbie sighed with pleasure. Now the girls had something to do. They couldn't go Mayflowering this spring, but they would be gathering crabs and sea moss.

Mrs. Burgess coached the children in their studies that evening, while Mr. Burgess pored over the Rockland newspapers. Now and then, he would interrupt Benjy's work to read aloud some political item he favored.

Abbie's thoughts kept roaming back to the letter she'd gotten from Prissy. Finally, she unfolded it again.

Lydia remarked, "Abbie must be homesick for Rockland. She keeps reading that letter."

"I don't miss Rockland," Abbie insisted. "I just miss Prissy —a little."

"Well, I miss all sorts of things," Lydia declared. "School and friends, and all those curios in Mr. Pratt's store." When her father cocked an eye at her, Lydia quickly added, "But I like it here on the Rock, Father. My ambition is to sketch the sunset with the lighthouse silhouetted against it."

Esther and Mahala took turns telling what they missed about Rockland. Abbie soon found herself saying, "I miss the library most. I've read all our books so many times, I practically know them by heart."

Mr. Burgess looked up again. "Write that down on our supply list, Thankful. I'll have Benjy buy some books for Abbie. The others can grow up to them."

Mrs. Burgess looked distressed. "Are you sending him back to Rockland again? He went just the other day——"

"That was a week ago, Thankful. We're obliged to get the barrels of lobsters to market regularly every week—or we lose a week's work." He turned to Abbie. "Tomorrow while I'm cleaning the lamps, you can go out with Ben and gather the catch."

"Whatever you say, Father," Abbie replied. "Lydia, you'll have to iron for me. I dampened the clothes today."

"Lydia and I will tend to the ironing," her mother said. "The lobstering buys provisions for us—so that comes first."

Dressed in one of Benjy's oilskins, a greased apron that hung nearly to her ankles, Abbie leaned against the side of the *Provider* while Benjy maneuvered the boat alongside one of the wooden boxes, or "cars," that floated about in the sparkling waves. The day before, Benjy and his father had emptied dozens of lobster traps and stored the catch in the cars.

The lobsters would keep only a day or two atop the water, so the cars had to be emptied today. Then they'd still be fresh for Benjy to take to market. Every one that arrived in Rockland alive meant fruit, fresh milk, yarn for knitting, woolen cloth for winter clothes, and medicine for Mother.

It pleasured Abbie to be on the water, but she'd never felt so pulled between responsibilities. Tied to the rope, she knew that Mahala couldn't get into mischief. But what was Esther up to? And how was Lydia faring with the ironing? She wondered if her mother would overwork herself and have another of her spells.

"Keep the boat steady, Sis!" Benjy called to her. With the gaff, he hooked the end of a box and pulled it toward the dory.

Abbie feathered the oars to keep the dory in position while Benjy lifted the box into the boat. He opened the wooden hinge on the box as he set it down on the seat, saying at the same time, "There's some more work for you."

She made her way across the dory, balancing herself against the lift of the waves. Benjy grinned at her. "Didn't take you long to find your sea legs, did it, Sis?"

He turned back to the oars and while he sculled along to another car, Abbie transferred the thrashing greenish-black lobsters from the box to one of the barrels. Whenever she got a whiff of the basket of rotten fish Benjy used to bait the traps, she remembered her father telling Lydia that as long as the wind was in the other direction, the smell wasn't so dreadful. But it was vile enough to force Abbie to take deep gulps of fresh sea air whenever she could.

In an hour, they had emptied all the cars. "Now," Benjy said, "we'll collect the traps, so I can take today's catch along, too. Get ready, there's a buoy up ahead——"

She had quickly learned that a red-and-white buoy marked the location of several lobster traps. Each buoy was precious, for Benjy had spent many hours cutting the small objects from logs that had drifted up with the tide, and Lydia had painted them in artistic stripes of red and white.

"Grab the gaff, Abbie—quick now."

She picked up the pole with the hook on the end and pulled the buoy toward her. Benjy leaned over the side of the dory and tugged at the rope until a wooden lobster trap appeared on the surface. More rope emerged, then another trap, another length of rope, and finally the last trap came up. He hauled it all up into the boat.

He stacked them on the seat, then opened them carefully. Pulling out several crabs, he tossed them into one basket; the lobsters into another. He speared a piece of rotting fish, threaded it on the bait string, refastened the trap, and then moved on to the next trap with such speed that Abbie marveled at his skill. He picked up the oars again, and began to row along, leaving Abbie to push the traps back into the water.

On their way back to the Rock, Abbie said, "Now that you're lobstering and sailing to Rockland every week, I suppose you'll be changing your mind about leaving."

Benjy shook his head. "You and Mother are more set on keeping me here than Father is. If I could stay out in the boat all day, I wouldn't mind the Rock. Abbie, I'm really in a mess. We'll be lobstering clear into October, and if I wait until then to leave, there won't be much fishing, unless I go South—far South."

"Oh, Benjy, I can't bear the thought of your leaving. I know you want that kind of life, but I'll miss you something dreadful."

Benjy smiled at her in a tender way. "Not for long, Sis. You'll be busy about the lighthouse doing things you enjoy. Here comes another buoy—grab the gaff."

Abbie poked the gaff into the water and caught the corner of another striped buoy. She'd never felt so helpless before. She could keep house and cook; she could do her share of woman's work, even man's work, but she couldn't persuade her brother to stay. She figured he'd inherited too much of their father's restless nature. As much as she'd miss Benjy, though, Abbie was sure the worst part of his leaving would be consoling their mother.

CHAPTER IX

Benjy Leaves

ABBIE HAD never imagined a day on the Rock could pass so slowly. She'd helped her father with the lamps, done many other chores in the afternoon, and now there was some chowder simmering on the stove for supper. But the cutter that was due to bring Prissy, as well as their monthly supplies, still hadn't arrived.

"Prissy's gone and changed her mind," Esther declared.

Mahala grinned impishly as she said, "I suspect she's found a new beau."

Lydia glanced up from the dishes she was washing. "Abbie, I can't figure why you invited Prissy for two whole days. She won't have a speck of fun. She'll probably swim all the way back to Rockland."

"Prissy can't swim a dab," Abbie replied. "And you all know the supply boat never comes on time."

Mrs. Burgess appeared, smiling brightly. "The suspense is over, Abigail. A boat's offshore. Your father's on his way to the landing."

Abbie hurried out, her sisters trailing behind as she made her way across the Rock. Heat rose from its surface, but the breeze skimming across the ocean fanned it away.

When she reached the ledge, Abbie brushed off her skirt and tucked wisps of hair under her braid. Prissy would surely take notice if she wasn't looking ladylike.

Her father was shouting to the man on the cutter as it came alongside the Rock, and Prissy was at the railing, waving to them.

"She's certainly fancied up," Lydia said. "Even got a pink parasol to match her dress."

"That's Prissy," Abbie declared. "But I didn't think she'd wear such fine clothes for this trip."

"Just setting eyes on her makes me wish I was back in Rockland," Lydia added wistfully.

Some of the crew lowered a tender, and one of the men helped Prissy down the ladder and into the boat. He rowed closer to the shore and waited there until two breakers had rolled in; then he rowed in on the crest of the third one. He threw a rope toward Mr. Burgess, who began to pull the boat onto the ways.

Suddenly, Prissy got to her feet, waving and shouting excitedly.

"*Sit down!*" Abbie yelled. Everyone was motioning for Prissy to settle back in the boat, but Prissy didn't seem to notice. A wave swept the boat forward, and she lost her balance, toppled out of the boat, and fell face down in the water. She came up thrashing and screaming, her wet hair covering her eyes.

"Sakes' alive!" Abbie cried. Beside her, Mahala and Esther were jumping about, laughing and squealing all at once.

"Look at Prissy floundering," Lydia exclaimed in disgust. "Everybody's laughing at her—— Oh, Abbie, Father's reaching for her with the lobster gaff!"

"I'd best go to her," Abbie called back, already on her way down the stone steps. She reached the rocks at the water's edge just as her father hauled Prissy in.

The ruffles on her dress were limp, and her golden hair was as soggy as the seaweed under her feet.

"I was set on looking so elegant for you," Prissy wailed, "but now I'm a—a disaster!"

"You look fine," Abbie said as she welcomed her friend. "We'll have you dry in no time."

Mr. Burgess put down Prissy's valise. "I'll carry this up to the house later—after I get our supplies off the boat."

Lydia skipped ahead, the mail clutched in her hand. The younger girls hovered around Abbie, listening eagerly to Prissy's chatter.

"Oh, Abbie, I admire your Rock and your lighthouse. The sky seems bluer out here, and the water clearer, somehow. I've never laid my eyes on so many gulls!"

The girls pointed out the Rock birds and the terns, and vied with one another for Prissy's attention. But when they coaxed her toward the fog bell, Abbie shushed them.

"There'll be plenty of time to show Prissy everything. Right now, she needs to change her clothes and rest for a spell."

They moved on to the bottom of the kitchen steps. "What do you think of our house, Prissy? Is it strong enough to suit you?"

Prissy's gaze quietly measured its height and width. "Why, Abbie, it's as solid as the Rock itself."

As they entered the kitchen, they found Mrs. Burgess lying

on the floor. *"Mother!"* Abbie shrieked, hurrying to her. "Quick, Lydia, get her smelling salts. Esther—fetch me a wet towel."

It had been quite a while since Mother had fainted, so Abbie dared not think what it might mean. She held the salts under her mother's nose until she opened her eyes.

"Prissy," Mrs. Burgess moaned, "you're safe!"

The girls exchanged puzzled glances. "Prissy just missed her footing," Abbie said, "and fell into the water——"

Mrs. Burgess sighed. "I saw her climb down the ladder, and into the tender—then, before I could tell what happened, she was bobbing up and down in the ocean. I was sure she'd drown."

Abbie made some weak tea with milk for all of them. The girls helped to serve it, along with the ginger cakes Abbie had made especially for Prissy's visit. By then, Prissy had changed clothes and fastened her damp hair back with a velvet band.

Sitting at the kitchen table, their guest told them about the goings on in Rockland. She described the fancy lobby of the new hotel. She thrilled Lydia with details of the elegant dresses just imported from Paris and with stories of Mrs. Haskell's growing business. She gave the younger girls bits of news about their old school chums.

Abbie was pleased to see how quickly her mother perked up, and wasn't surprised to hear her say, "It's so good to have someone to neighbor with after all these months."

After a while, Abbie led Prissy upstairs to the bedrooms. Mahala ran ahead of them and climbed up into one of the wide-silled windows. "If you sit up here, Prissy," she said, "you can watch the ocean splash and roll. Abbie says it's a sight that never tires you."

Prissy exclaimed over the view and expressed delight over

Abbie's private bedroom. They chatted on as Prissy unpacked her valise.

Later, Abbie took her friend on a tour of the Rock, showing her all the spots the girls enjoyed and their favorite views of the sun-drenched water.

It was fun to have Prissy there, to chat about the past, and speculate about the future. That night, they took turns brushing one another's long hair. Abbie's light-brown tresses hung past her shoulders, but Prissy's golden hair reached her waistline.

Under the coverlet at last, Prissy told Abbie about the diary she was keeping. "But it's so dull," she confessed. "I don't want to remember the year I'm sixteen just for my dresses and parties and beaus. I wish something *dramatic* would happen to me sometime——"

"Like falling into the ocean?"

"Oh, Abbie, don't tease. I thought you'd have a lonely life out here, and you do in some ways. But you have excitement, too. You really should keep a diary, Abbie."

"I do—only I call it a log. I record whatever is unusual about each day. But nothing really exceptional has happened, so far."

"Well, if *I* were in your place, Abbie, I'd keep it up—just in case I became famous one day."

Abbie sneaked out of bed the next morning, trying not to wake Prissy who was sleeping so soundly she didn't stir when a gull screamed outside. At the open window, Abbie took a deep breath of the salt-scented air. She'd longed to show Prissy how beautiful the Rock could be, and the weather had not let her down.

She fixed breakfast for herself and her father, and then they worked on the lamps. When they were climbing down the steps of the second tower, Mr. Burgess said, "When Benjy comes back today, we'll be obliged to mend some traps so we can have a big catch this week while the market's good."

Abbie could hardly wait to have Benjy and Prissy joking together again. She just knew this would be a perfect day.

In the early afternoon, the four girls took Prissy down to their special spot above the cove, spread an old quilt, and stretched out on it.

They laughed at the antics of the colorful Rock birds, watched the gulls cracking and eating mussels, sighted several porpoises, and giggled over Sammy, the pet seal, when he appeared near the Rock. In her excitement, Prissy forgot her delicate complexion, laid aside her parasol, and let the sun touch her face.

Suddenly, Mahala shrieked, "There's a dory offshore, Abbie! It must be Benjy——"

The girls quickly hastened down to the landing site, except for Esther, who went to tell their father.

"Benjy is so brave," Prissy declared, as they stood on the shore and watched him heading in. "I admire his sailing all the way to Rockland alone."

They waited patiently until two breakers rolled in. Then, on the crest of the third, Benjy rowed forward, maneuvering the dory straight onto the ways. He threw a rope to Abbie, who pulled the boat farther up on the ways.

Benjy climbed out, his sandy hair tousled, his face deeply tanned from hours in the open sun. He tweaked a strand of Prissy's long hair. "So you forgot you don't like to fish or sail and came to visit us after all."

"Now, Benjy, it pleasures me to come see Abbie—to see all of you."

Benjy grinned. "You'll change your mind if I ever take you lobstering with me."

"You daren't, Benjy," Esther interrupted. "She'll fall right out of the boat!"

Reminded of the spectacle Prissy had made of herself the day before, Abbie and her sisters laughed again. It was Prissy, with blushing cheeks, who told Benjy how she had come to such a pass. After her recital, Benjy and Prissy kept on chattering, and Abbie fairly glowed with contentment.

Just before sunset, Benjy came into the kitchen. "Abbie," he said, "I'm burdened with a decision, and it's up to you to help me."

Abbie left Prissy with Lydia, who was sharing the secrets of her button collection, and went with Benjy to light the lamps. She guessed what he had to tell her, but she didn't want to hear the words.

"Sis, you remember that you promised to stand up for me? Well, the time has come. A fishing fleet put in at Rockland today because one of their men took sick. I talked with the captain. If I can get back by late morning, that man's job is mine."

"Oh, Benjy——" A cold chill passed over Abbie. "Have you spoken to Father?"

"I'd rather wait until after supper. But I've got to get it settled so I can get some sleep if I'm to shove off in the morning. Sis, my future's in your hands. If you don't convince Father you can tend the lamps, he won't give in."

Abbie promised to give thought to the matter. She wished

Benjy hadn't picked this time to fight for his independence, but she supposed there was no way to stop him from reaching out for a man's horizons.

After supper, while Abbie and her sisters cleared away the dishes, Mr. Burgess sat down at the table with the newspapers that had come on the supply boat. Benjy took a chair opposite him.

"Father," Benjy said right out, "I'm going to join a fishing fleet tomorrow." He hastened to explain how he'd heard about the opening, and that he must return to Rockland by forenoon tomorrow if he was to get the job. "It's a mother ship with twelve little dories. We'll sail to Bay Chaleur, near the St. Lawrence River, just below the Gaspé Peninsula in Canada."

Mr. Burgess stroked his beard. "I know those waters. They're rich in cod and mackerel. I've known men who've fished them, and my bones can feel the hardships you'll have to bear. But there's no need to live that kind of life. If you'll stay here, I'm bound to get you appointed my assistant."

"But you don't rightly need me, Father. Abbie can tend the lamps as well as anyone. I'll send some money back, and by next summer, Lydia will be grown enough to help with the lobstering."

When Lydia's name was spoken, she blurted, "Father, I'll knit heads, and polish brass—but I'll *never* set foot on a lobster boat!"

Mrs. Burgess, who had been hiding tears behind a handkerchief, now said, "You're not full grown, Benjy. And you're our only son. Your father needs your strength and your sisters need your courage."

Benjy looked sullen. "I reckon I'm selfish and irresponsible, but my heart's set on fishing. Father went to sea when he was a boy, so why is it so wrong for me?"

"I know the dangers," Mrs. Burgess said, "that's why *I'm* against it. Walk down any street in Rockland, and you'll meet many widows and orphans of the men who went to sea."

"But a heap of those men were lost on clippers and whalers," Benjy protested. "We're not likely to be caught in a storm so far out that no one could rescue us." His eyes brightened as he told how it would be. "Every morning at sunup I'll go out in a dory, bait my hooks, drop my line, and then row around for several hours. In the afternoon, I'll haul in my line, take my catch off the hooks, then row back to the mother ship for the night. It's easy," he assured them, "long's the weather's good. If there's a fog, it might take a spell to find my way back, but the mother ship is well lighted, so I'll have no trouble getting my bearings."

Mr. Burgess laid his newspaper aside. "Son, the sea's satisfying to a man because it challenges him to prove his manhood. But the ocean is a demon when it's angry. Only a fool says he has no fear of it. It's the men who ignore and defy the ocean's warnings that seldom live to boast about it."

Benjy shifted restlessly. "Father, there are dangers in any kind of work."

"He's right, Father," Abbie said. "You've taught us to accept adventure and danger as part of our natural lives. We've no right to keep Benjy from the thing he loves most."

"Aye," Mr. Burgess agreed. "I know Ben will never be content until he gets the sea out of his blood." His eyes went from her to Mrs. Burgess. "It's Mother I'm thinking about."

The time had come for Abbie to say her speech. "None of us wants to see Benjy leave, Father. We love him dearly. But he must have a chance to make his way on his own. I can do Benjy's work here. I'll take his place—I'll be your assistant."

Abbie noticed Prissy's look of dismay and her mother's sad face. But her spirits lifted when her father said, at last, "We've been at loggerheads about this long enough, Son. It's time you had your way."

Abbie went with Benjy down to the landing before dawn the next morning, carrying a basket of lunch over her arm. Up ahead, their father swung a lantern. "Do write often, Benjy," she said, "for Mother's sake."

"I'll try. And whenever we put into port, I'll buy some trinkets and send them along."

They'd just reached the stone steps when someone shouted behind them. They turned and saw Prissy running toward them, her robe flashing blue in the dim light.

"Abbie," she cried, "why didn't you wake me? I wanted to see Benjy off, too. Here——" she pressed something into Benjy's hand. "Take this penny with you to remember me by. Maybe it'll make the fish bite more often."

"A lucky penny," Benjy said, sounding pleased as he thanked her. "I'll keep it until I come back. If you haven't caught yourself a husband by then, maybe I'll bring you something fancy."

Abbie had never taken well to good-bys, and this was surely the saddest one she'd ever known, for she sensed that once Benjy was free of them he was not likely to return for a very long time.

CHAPTER X

Abbie and Her Hens

SUMMER PASSED and a spell of autumn came. The daylight grew shorter, the lamps burned more oil, and now in October, the sting of the wind foretold an early winter.

Abbie missed watching foliage changing from green to brown and gold, but she took pleasure in the shifting tides, and the varying moods of the ocean. She felt obliged now to measure up to Benjy's strength. She could climb about the towers as light and easy as the gulls at play, but she felt weak and gawky helping her father trap lobsters or haul up the dory. The summer waters had yielded such a bounty of lobsters that her father had sailed to Rockland every Monday with several barrels of them, each time taking a list of the things the girls and their mother wanted him to buy with the money the lobsters brought.

Abbie had never been so frightened as she was that first time he'd sailed away, leaving her in charge of the lighthouse for two days. But the hardest work was soothing her mother's fears. Still, she couldn't blame her mother. With no menfolk around, even Abbie fell to wondering what might happen if that emergency her father spoke about should occur.

Each time she lighted the lamps, though, her confidence grew. And each time her father left for Rockland, Mother fretted less, just as she now spoke Benjy's name only occasionally.

One night, when the girls were sitting about the kitchen table doing their handiwork, Mahala mentioned Benjy, and Mrs. Burgess declared, "I'm growing resigned to it now. I'll never see my Benjy again."

It was then that Abbie said, "Mother, we're all saddened every time we see his empty chair at the table. But Benjy loves us—second only to the sea. He'll come back."

Mrs. Burgess smiled. "Abigail, I didn't mean we'd never see him again. I'm saying that when we lay eyes on him, it won't be our Benjy. He'll be a man grown."

"And handsome," Esther said. "I wonder if he'll have a beard—like Father's?"

Just the day before, Mr. Burgess had gone to Rockland with the last haul of the lobster season. Abbie felt so burdened by her numerous duties that she had tried to put Lydia to cleaning the lamps that morning. Lydia had climbed halfway up the first tower, turned sick at the smell of the oil, and fled in disgust. Since she couldn't depend on her sister for lighthouse work, Abbie decided it was high time she learned more woman's work.

Coming down from the second tower, she stopped at the door where Lydia was shining an oil can. "You must help Mother fix supper," Abbie told her. "I can't tend to that and the lamps."

"Well, I can't traipse around the kitchen and keep the brass shining, too."

"We're all obliged to work hard, Lydia. If the place isn't in good repair, the inspector will send in a bad report on Father."

"An inspector!" Lydia wrinkled her nose. "We've been here six months, and one hasn't set foot on the place yet. I don't believe there *is* such a thing."

"Father says they visit the station every four months or so, and we must be ready."

Esther and Mahala scurried about their morning chores. Later in the day, they brought down their dolls and played on the back steps where the sun was warmest. While Abbie and Lydia did the ironing, Mrs. Burgess sat in her rocker, busy with a lapful of mending.

"Lydia's nearly outgrown her coat, Abigail. It's time we made a new one for you, so Lydia can have yours. I hope your father finds some shoes for the little ones. Mercy, how those rocks wear leather down."

Just then, Abbie heard her sisters shouting outside. She ran to the back door and flung it open. Mahala and Esther were hurrying toward the landing where a white sail billowed above the gray water.

"It's the cutter!" Abbie turned to her mother in surprise. "It was here just a week ago——"

"Must be the inspector," Mrs. Burgess mused. "Oh dear, of all times—when the men are away."

Abbie shuddered. "Whoever it is, I'd best be meeting them." She threw on her shawl and set out, holding her skirt against the wind. When she caught up with her sisters, Mahala asked, "Is Father coming back on the cutter?"

"Not likely," Abbie replied. She stood on the ledge with the two girls while the breakers rolled in, worrying over who was coming to the Rock. When she glimpsed the man in uniform leaning on the railing of the cutter, her heart fairly sank.

"Abbie," Esther whispered, "he looks a lot like an inspector."

"That *is* the inspector!" She recognized the uniform from a photograph she'd seen in one of the booklets about the lighthouse service that were kept in the lamp room.

By the time she reached the ways, the crew had lowered a tender into the water. One of the men began to row over to the shore with the inspector. He shouted to Abbie, asking where her father might be.

"He's in Rockland," she called back above the pounding of the waves. "Toss your rope; I'll bring you in."

She got the boat up a few feet, and the inspector climbed out. He gave the tender a shove, and the other man headed back to the cutter. The visitor stepped up to Abbie. "Good afternoon, Miss. I'm the inspector from the Lighthouse Board. I presume you're one of the Burgess children——"

With a curtsy, Abbie introduced herself. "My father sailed for Rockland yesterday forenoon with a lobster catch. He'll be back by sunset."

The inspector frowned. "I didn't calculate on the Keeper being gone. I must make my inspection before the cutter returns."

"I'm my father's helper," Abbie explained. "I can tend the lamps for him if he has to be away. I'd be pleasured to show you about."

"Indeed." His dark eyes fastened on her as if he didn't

believe it. "Well," he said, "I'll admit you handled that boat right well—almost like a man."

They mounted the stone steps together, and Abbie assured him he'd find everything shipshape. The girls, she noticed, had already dashed back to the house to alert their mother and Lydia about the visitor.

Walking beside him, Abbie could see that he was already inspecting. He peered into the boathouse, noting the tidy shelves and the rope coiled neatly in the corners. He walked on to the fog bell and inspected the rope and the poles. From there, he went to the nearest tower, opened the outside door, and stepped inside.

While they were going up the steps of the tower, he asked many questions. Abbie proudly told him that she was nearly fifteen. "And I'm strong," she added. "My brother Benjy thinks I'm mighty sturdy for a girl."

Though the inspector agreed with that, it was his opinion that she was too young to be left in charge of a lighthouse station.

"But my mother's here, too. She's probably setting out tea for us this very minute."

He stopped on the landing. Using the light from the window above, he opened a small ledger and read from it. "I don't have any record of an assistant having been appointed on Matinicus Rock."

"It isn't likely that my mother ever will be, Sir. She's frail and sickly. Climbing these stairs every day would be too much for her."

Inside the lamp room, he examined the lamps, the oil cans, even the windows. On the way down the stairs, he asked, "How often does your father go to Rockland, Miss Abigail?"

"Nearly every week, since my brother left." She proceeded

to tell him how sorely they needed the money they earned from the lobsters and how, right in the middle of the season, Benjy had left. "So now I'm obliged to help Father with all the work."

They went up into the second tower, and Abbie stood aside while the inspector examined the place. "Before I can put approval on my report, I'd like to see how you light one of these lamps."

Abbie was taken aback, but she was eager to prove to him that she could do things properly. She lifted the glass chimney off the nearest lamp, and set it down. She went through the procedure of lighting the wick and then put the chimney back in place. The inspector smiled his approval.

He seemed quite concerned about how far the lamps shone through the dark. Abbie could only say, "Father was told it's about fifteen miles."

"It should be farther," he replied. "Much farther."

Abbie then took the inspector into the house and introduced him to her mother, who graciously served tea. While her sisters were showing off their samplers to the guest, Abbie silently prayed that her mother wouldn't let on how insecure she felt on the Rock when her husband was away. Abbie thought the inspector felt satisfied that her mother was here, believing the two of them could operate the light station efficiently.

His visit finally over, he said, "I've never seen this station looking so comfortable, Mrs. Burgess. You've a real knack for making it homelike."

Abbie fairly skipped as she went back to the landing with the inspector. There she waited with him until the cutter came alongside the Rock.

Before he left, he said, "You may tell your father, Miss

Abigail, that when I set foot on Matinicus Light Station today and found a young girl in charge, I intended to report Sam Burgess as negligent in his duties. It would surely have cost him his appointment. But after meeting you and your mother, I feel Matinicus Rock is in good hands. Very good hands, indeed."

Abbie was still in high spirits when her father returned, climbed out of the dory, and asked about her day. The girls clustered around, telling him all about the inspector.

"Now *there's* a fine kettle of fish! I reckon he'll report me for being away——"

"He had a mind to," Abbie said, "but I think he truly admires us now." She told him all that had happened.

Her father grinned broadly. "I've brought you a present, Daughter, and it's a fitting reward for what you've done for us all today."

He lifted a wooden crate from the dory, and strange cackling sounds drew Abbie over for a closer look. In between the slats, she saw moving, white-feathered forms.

"They're hens!" she exclaimed.

"Aye. Five of them. I figured they'd make fine pets for you, but I reckon the other girls will claim them."

"Abbie won't mind if we take one for our own," Lydia said. "Will you, Abbie?"

She shook her head. "How could I ever stop you from loving these little creatures?"

Mr. Burgess stacked more supplies on the shore. Then he toted the hen crate up to the house and placed it beside the kitchen steps. He put the sack of grain for the hens in the storeroom behind the kitchen.

Mrs. Burgess was as pleased as the girls over the little white hens. "Sam," she said at supper, "put the coop up there among the boulders. It's sunny there and close to the house, and the rocks will be a protection against the wind."

"What'll we name the hens?" Mahala wanted to know.

"That's Abbie's pleasure," Mr. Burgess replied.

"Then I'd like to wait," she told them, "until we make friends of the hens."

The girls chased the little creatures about the Rock for several days while Mr. Burgess built a large wooden coop and a small wire-fenced enclosure for them.

When he announced that the coop was ready, the girls collected the hens, placed them inside the fence, and then watched as Abbie conducted a ceremony befitting the occasion.

"After several days of observing them," she began, "it's best we give them names that suit their dispositions. This one, who is usually huddled in a snug spot, I name 'Peace.' This one, who is forever poking about for a tasty bite, I name 'Hope.' " She picked up the third one. "This dear little thing should be called 'Charity' because she lets the others share her findings. And this poor thing, who drags along behind, taking what is left, should rightly be named 'Patience.' "

She reached out for the fifth hen, saying, "But this one— with the patch of dark feathers on each side—who's more flighty than the others, I now name 'Priscilla.' "

Amid the merry laughter, Esther spoke up, "I recollect when Prissy said she'd never live on a lighthouse station. And here she is—right in our hen coop!"

CHAPTER XI

The Lighthouse Logs

WINTER CAME, and strong winds whipped across the Rock so fiercely that the girls spent their afternoons inside the house. Now they couldn't wave to sailors or ships that passed the Rock or count fishing boats. And the excursion boat that had brought a few visitors during the summer wouldn't operate until next season.

The little girls grew restless from the confinement and bickered more than usual. They cherished every toy and book they owned, and made quite a ceremony each day out of feeding and fondling the hens.

Abbie was grateful that her mother was bearing Benjy's absence so well. But now she began to stay in her room for hours with the door closed, and when Abbie asked her about it, her mother would explain that she was just "resting a spell."

Mahala spent a lot of time with her nose pressed against the windowpane, hoping to sight a boat offshore. She was there again the afternoon the cutter made its November visit to the Rock. "It's the supply boat," she exclaimed, "really and truly!"

Abbie helped the girls into their coats and mufflers, and hurried outside with them. They stood on the ledge, admiring the boat and listening to their father talking with the men as they unloaded the barrels of rations.

One of the men came up the steps and handed a bundle of mail to Abbie. She pulled out a letter that bore Benjy's handwriting, and Esther went to the house to give it to their mother.

After a while, they all huddled around the Boston rocker while Mrs. Burgess read the letter aloud:

" 'Dear Family: I am well. I have my own dory and a hundred hooks on my lines. Some of the men have sailed the globe, so I have some exciting tales to bring home, but that won't be very soon. I hope all are well. Keep the lights burning, Abbie. And Mother, I hope you and Father have forgiven me for leaving at such a time. Am sending a package for Abbie, to thank her for taking my part. Next time, I'll send something for each of you.' "

Mr. Burgess brought the package in, and Abbie stretched out the pleasure of opening it as long as her sisters allowed. When she picked up the delicate linen with its dainty embroidery work, she was flustered. "It's a tablecloth—but I don't even have a hope chest!"

"I declare." Mrs. Burgess fingered it carefully. "Must have set him back a week's wages."

"Now, Thankful," Mr. Burgess said, "he's bound to spend his wages. Might as well buy something useful. Abbie will never get a finer cloth than this one, I'm sure."

It touched her deeply to have Benjy think of her in such a

way. Smiling, she shook the cloth out and held it up for all to admire.

"Where will you keep it?" Lydia asked. "You don't have a hope chest, and there's not a speck of room left in the blanket chest."

Mrs. Burgess spoke up then. "Sam, it's time Abigail started a hope chest. She's going on fifteen. In my day, girls were setting things by long before her age."

"Next time I go to Rockland," Abbie's father promised, "I'll buy some fine wood and make her a chest."

All the fuss about the tablecloth and hope chest helped Abbie to forget her disappointment over getting no letter from Prissy. But there were several newspapers which Abbie looked forward to reading, for she and her father often discussed political developments and world events.

The wind howled about the house so loudly that Mr. Burgess decided to batten things down earlier than usual. He'd taught Abbie that, far out as they were, a gale could strike at any time during the winter season. He set great store by the barometer readings and consulted them often. He poured whale oil from the hogsheads into the smaller cans every day, for he believed that the more precautions they took, the more likely they'd weather a storm safely.

Though such precautions made Abbie feel safer, they aroused fear in her mother. Abbie encouraged her father, during his nightly devotional, to read certain passages in the Bible that concerned faith, hoping they would comfort her mother. They seemed to—at least for the moment.

Now that she could light the lamps with as much skill as her father, Abbie looked forward to her visits to the towers. Even though the wind shrieked around the towers menacingly, and the sea lashed the Rock with a dreadful booming sound, inside the lamp rooms, she felt cozy and safe.

One of the Keeper's duties was to make an entry in the lighthouse log—a leather-bound ledger—recording the events of each day: any unusual weather conditions, problems with the lights, boats sighted, rescues. Abbie's father made a hasty note each morning, but she wished he'd honor the logs more and mark down such things as the days the supply boat came and the times the inspector made his visits.

One morning after she finished cleaning the lamps, she discovered an old ledger lying behind one of the oil cans. She pulled it out, lifted it up to the circular shelf, and opened it. As she began to read, she realized that she'd come across one of the earliest logs of Matinicus Light Station, for the first entries were dated back in 1829. Her eyes widened as she read the words:

3 Sept. 1829 A heavy gail [gale] of wind to NW
31 Oct. 1829 a severe gail broak [broke] over Rock
9 Nov. 1829 a bad storm
24 Nov. 1829 a man-of-war passed here today
25 Jan. 1830 vilant [violent] snow storm
30 Jan. 1830 a sataday [Saturday] night, very cold
9 Feb. 1830 trim and set up all night
21 Feb. 1830 schooner passed here today
23 May 1830 the keeper very sick
10 June 1830 the keeper is better and he ought to be

There were other interesting comments. On October 11, 1832, the Keeper wrote: "125 sail in sight." In March 1833, "Went from and to the Rock 5 days this month." April

16, 1833, had this line, "Caught 6 codfish. The first for the year."

Abbie smiled when she read the entry of June 11, 1833: "Keeper measured Matinicus Rock and found it according to his figuring 2350 feet long, 567 feet wide, 34 and %10 acres."

She found more ledgers in the tower and decided to read them straight through and up to the present. As she read the logs, she found more and more fascinating entries. But over the weeks, she became more concerned with the records of the winters. Several times waves as high as thirty feet had splashed over the entire Rock.

She knew the storm of 1827 had washed away the first lighthouse, which had been built that very year. She found no record of a storm since then that had been as severe.

By Thanksgiving, she'd read as far as 1839 in the old logs. One morning she came to an entry in a water-stained ledger dated January 27, 1839, which recounted a storm, during which seven successive breakers, rising nearly forty feet in the air, had completely covered the Rock. The house had been carried away, but the Keeper and his family escaped in a dory. After a night of tossing about on the wild sea, they were picked up by a schooner and taken to the mainland.

Abbie decided that event accounted for the ledger being water-stained. The Keeper had undoubtedly taken the log with him, feeling duty bound to preserve the records of the lighthouse. She was puzzled as to why she'd never heard about that storm, for it sounded much worse than the one of 1827. She began to suspect that her father knew of it, but had kept it to himself in order not to worry her mother.

Now she felt obliged to read the rest of the logs, to learn if there had been another, later storm as terrible as the one in

1839. She turned page after page, skipping to the wintry seasons. Her eyes began to smart and her back felt stiff from leaning over the ledger. But her mind was set on knowing exactly what was in store for them. Had the officials at the Lighthouse Board warned her father about the severity of the storms that were apt to hit the Rock? She couldn't rest until she'd asked him.

That evening, after the others had gone to bed, she said, "Father, I've been reading the old logs in the tower. Why didn't you tell me there'd been so many storms?"

"Now, there's no need to get alarmed. Only two storms were violent enough to cause damage and then it was only to the wooden towers and dwellings. They finally built this granite house in 1848, with the towers at each end. Some of the finest Army engineers constructed it, so it'll be here for quite a spell."

Abbie felt greatly relieved, for, as her father went on, she knew he'd been fully informed about the Rock. There was, however, one fear she couldn't wipe away. "Father, I'm wondering about the wooden chamber you and Mother use for a bedroom. If a storm is violent enough—couldn't it wash away?"

He drew a long puff on his pipe. "Aye. But if a storm's abrewing, we'll have time to move your mother into the parlor—and the furniture, to boot."

At last, Abbie felt at peace. She had no reason to doubt that the house would endure, but she decided to keep the contents of the logs to herself. If her mother learned of some of the entries, she'd take to her bed for certain!

CHAPTER XII

A Christmas Guest

A FEW DAYS before Christmas, Abbie rose early and, as was her custom, looked out of the window. She almost shrieked in delight. The light from the towers shone against a shimmering sheet of white snow. She awakened her sisters so they could admire the sight. They leaned drowsily against the windows for a moment, then moaned about having no sleds to play with, and crawled back into bed.

Abbie went downstairs and started breakfast, her mind crowded with questions about the effect snow would have on their lighthouse work. She could see her father outside in his snowshoes, shoveling a path from the kitchen steps to the sheds and the outhouses. She hoped he'd already scraped the snow off the lighthouse windows.

He came in soon, stamping his boots as he draped his coat on a chair beside the crackling fire.

"Well," he said in a tone of resignation, "the girls will have to do without their Christmas tree. I can't sail in this weather. There's more shoveling to do, and I calculate there'll be more snow."

"Don't mind about the tree, Father. We'll have a good Christmas just the same." As long as Abbie could remember, the Burgesses had made a big fuss about Christmas. This year it had been a challenge to see how festive they could make the occasion without relying on supplies from the mainland. For months, they'd been so busy on private projects, especially during the hour after supper, that they'd come to call it the "secret hour."

Abbie served a breakfast of salt pork, biscuits, preserves, hot tea, and pumpkin pie. After they'd eaten, her father went back to his shoveling. Abbie climbed the towers, blew out the lamps, and cleaned them. Snow was still falling, so she went out on the catwalk and brushed the corners of the windows; then she swept a layer of fine white powder off the catwalk itself.

From that height, the Rock was a strange sight. It was white, but out beyond the ledges, breakers rolled in, as gray and noisy as ever.

She went back to the kitchen and began another batch of cookies. For weeks now, before the girls awoke in the morning or after they went to bed at night, she'd baked cookies, stored them in a crock, and hid them behind the flour barrel in the storeroom.

The supply boat hadn't made its December trip, and since her father wouldn't be going to the mainland, she'd have no more raisins or nuts, and now spices were getting low. She'd have to settle for making simple sugar cookies this morning. There were some chestnuts left from her father's last shopping trip in Rockland that could be roasted in the hot coals in the fireplace.

Soon, the girls came downstairs, dressed for the day.

"I smell something good," Esther said, sniffing.

"Like cinnamon," Mahala added. "Did you make a surprise for us, Abbie?"

"If I tell you, it won't be a surprise, will it?"

Lydia wrinkled her nose. "Cookies won't take the place of the tree Father planned to get. I can't abide this weather, Abbie! First, the wind was too strong for him to sail; then it was so cold he was afraid ice would form on the boat. And now it's snowing. And what's worse—there's not even a bush on the Rock we could use for a tree. We're just marooned out here!"

Mrs. Burgess joined them in time to chide Lydia for her outburst. "We all have good reason to wish your father could make the trip," she said. "But we're obliged to make the best of things."

"But it won't be Christmas without a tree!" Mahala cried.

Mrs. Burgess quietly sipped her tea. "Children, people have been celebrating Christmas for years without putting up a tree. It's a fairly new custom here in America. Why, Abbie and Benjy never saw one until they were your age, Esther. Now, clean your plates. After chores, we'll make some snow ice cream. There's a bucket of maple syrup just begging to be dribbled over some fresh snow."

The snow added beauty and pleasure to their Christmas season, but it buried the various materials the younger girls had been gathering to make Christmas gifts. On autumn afternoons, Abbie had walked along the shore when the tide was out, while her sisters, a basket on each arm, picked up pretty shells and seaweed that had interesting shapes and sizes. Then they had slipped away to the workshop to paint and decorate the shells, dip the seaweed into whitewash, and glue things together. Lydia had kept to herself during those weeks, sketching. She'd taken possession of one of the trunks they'd brought and ordered the others not to open it.

Abbie quickly assured her sisters now that they had already made plenty of gifts for the entire family and that they'd have a grand holiday without a tree.

Before the morning was out, the snow had become as great an event as the arrival of the supply boat. The girls frolicked outside, the way they always had in Rockland. Though they had no hills to slide down or ponds to skate on, they enjoyed their snowshoes more than ever before.

During the afternoon, the wintry air suddenly turned warmer and fog set in. "It's too early for a thaw," Mr. Burgess explained to them at supper, "so the fog shouldn't last long. But the bell will have to be rung every ten or fifteen minutes, day and night, until the fog lifts. I can't do my other chores and ring the bell, too," he went on. "Any one of you three young girls could pull that rope all by herself."

"Oh, Father!" Lydia cried. "I don't want to spend my Christmas ringing that heavy old bell!"

"On a lighthouse station," Mr. Burgess reminded her, "our duty comes first. Abbie and I will be ringing it all night, so you girls will have to ring it and do most of her chores during the day so she can get some sleep. Lydia, you should be more grateful for the blessings you have."

"Don't think harshly of her, Sam," Mrs. Burgess interrupted. "She's grateful, just as we are, to have a snug home, good food, and warm clothes."

"Our girls don't know what real hardship is, Thankful. Not many years ago, these parts were overrun with Indians. Now we have good relations with the Indians—at least for the time being."

The girls trudged across the Rock and rang the fog bell during the early evening until their father took over. Then they helped Abbie clean the kitchen and immediately afterward got ready for bed. In their robes and slippers, they sat around the kitchen table and listened to their mother read from the Bible the story of the birth of Christ. When she promised to read it again the next night, they went willingly to bed.

On the third night after the snowfall, Abbie dressed warmly, strapped on a pair of snowshoes, and went out after supper to spell her father at the fog bell. It was the evening before Christmas Eve. For two nights and days they had been ringing the bell, sleeping whenever they could. She liked being outdoors. Though the warm current of air that had produced the fog had melted much of the snow, the air was cold enough to sharpen the salt smell and tingle her clear to her toes. There was no wind now, and the ocean was still.

She'd seen fog form a gray wall across the waterfront at Rockland, but she'd never felt so surrounded by it before. The lantern lighted only a patch of the fog as she headed in the direction of the bell. Once there, her father handed her the rope and left. She put her lantern down, pulled the rope firmly, and the bell boomed out across the water.

Somehow, the fog only made her miss Benjy more. She'd thought of Benjy a great deal lately. This would be their first Christmas without him, and it saddened her to think of it.

She brushed away some snow and sat down on a rock to rest before she rang the bell again. Suddenly she heard a voice calling, "Ahoy! Ahoy there, Matinicus!"

Her heart fairly leaped into her throat. Someone was

trying to land on the Rock! She hurried into the house to get her father, and they headed down to the landing. She marveled how he was able to keep his bearings all the way to the ledge, for she could hardly see her hand before her face.

Going down the stone steps, her father called out, "Keeper Burgess here! Where are you?"

"Father, it's me! Can you pull me in?"

"Benjy!" Abbie cried with joy. But her father didn't sound so pleased.

"Son, how could a seaman like you set out in a fog like this?"

"It was clear when I left Rockland at dawn. I had a good sail—until a couple of hours ago when I hit the fog. My hands are numb from rowing. Lucky that bell was ringing, or I'd have rowed past the Rock, for sure."

After Benjy's boat was up on the ways, they helped him unload his gear. On the bottom of the boat was a large pine tree. "I spent the night at Mr. Pratt's store," Benjy explained. "He told me he hadn't seen you around in a month, Father, so I figured you'd need some food—and a Christmas tree."

They walked slowly across the Rock, and Benjy told how his fleet had put into Boston for the holiday, and he had talked the captain into allowing him to sail to the Rock in the fishing dory.

It was a happy time for all. The girls were thrilled over the tree and Benjy's sack of gifts. After a hearty breakfast, he erected the stately pine in a corner of the kitchen, and the girls strung popcorn and hung it about decoratively.

Abbie brought out some of her cookies and fastened them

on the branches. Gifts were taken from their hiding places and placed beneath the tree. The final touch was the starfish Abbie had found last summer, dried, and now sprinkled with sugar so that it glistened in the glow from the lamp.

Mrs. Burgess was delighted with the turkey Benjy had brought. After months of fish, dried beef, and pork, fowl was a welcome change. And Abbie was relieved that Benjy had included nuts and spices in his sack. The girls begged some of the hard candies Mr. Pratt had generously added to the purchases.

Abbie and her mother dressed the turkey for roasting tomorrow, stewed cranberries, and made mince and pumpkin pies. Meanwhile, the menfolk went outside to keep their vigilance at the fog bell.

Sometime later, Abbie heard her father shouting for someone to open the kitchen door. She flung it open, and there were Benjy and her father supporting a young man between them. He was not much older than Benjy, Abbie noticed, and dark and slender. Blood was streaming down his face from a wound on his forehead.

The girls stood about gaping, while the stranger was half-carried to the couch.

"Thankful," Mr. Burgess directed, "get some of my clothes. Girls, hurry and fetch some blankets."

Benjy pulled off the young man's boots and set them aside, saying, "If we hadn't gone to see about my boat, he might have washed out at the turn of the tide. We barely heard him moaning. Hope his boat wasn't damaged beyond repair."

"Is he conscious?" Abbie asked.

"Reckon he was stunned when his boat crashed against the rocks," Mr. Burgess said. "He's coming around now."

The young seaman opened his eyes and looked at them all bewilderedly. Mahala, who'd been jumping about in great excitement, blurted, "This is Matinicus Light Station, and you're the first shipwrecked sailor we've rescued. This is my father—he's the Keeper."

"We're the Burgesses," Lydia added with a curtsy and a timid smile. "We're glad you dropped in." The others laughed and added their greetings.

The young man smiled feebly. "I'm glad to make your acquaintance. I'm Caleb Pendelton, out of Gloucester, Massachusetts. What happened to my boat?"

"Ben and I tied a line on her," Mr. Burgess replied, "and pulled her up out of the rocks. Soon's you're strong enough, we'll see what needs repairing."

After Mrs. Burgess bathed and bandaged the wound, Benjy helped Caleb into dry clothes. Then Abbie served him some food and hot tea.

Benjy soon had the young man explaining how he came to be there. "I ship aboard the *Mary Dee*. We were fishing off Rockland two days ago. When fog settled in, I was bound for my ship, but I strayed from my course. I knew Matinicus Light was somewhere hereabouts. I thought I heard a bell, but I couldn't figure just where it was sounding from. I drifted a while, then I guess I fell asleep from exhaustion. Next thing I knew, I had slammed into some rocks. They pushed up through the keel, and the blow hurled me back against the stern. Reckon that's when I struck my head."

Mr. Burgess stroked his beard thoughtfully. "You say you couldn't tell where the sound of the bell was coming from?"

"Not at first, Sir. And by the time I did figure it out, I was already upon the Rock—it was too late to avoid a crash."

"I've suspected that," Mr. Burgess said. "If this station's going to serve its purpose, the Lighthouse Board will be obliged to make some changes to the towers and the bell."

Benjy fell into a rapt discussion with Caleb about their experiences at sea. Neither of them liked the new steamships, which they considered noisy and dirty, and they both preferred the clean simplicity of sails. But they did admire the whaling ships, and they exchanged tales about them.

Abbie enjoyed hearing their talk, but she saw that her mother looked upset. "Mother," she said, "we'd best get on with the carols before it's time for the girls to go to bed." She laid another log on the fire, and the family drew closer to it and began to sing their favorite Christmas carols. Caleb, propped against pillows, smiled in pleasure. After Abbie passed around some cookies and spiced tea, he perked up even more.

With one last look at the Christmas tree, laden with gifts and good things, the girls finally trotted up to bed, giggling among themselves.

What a Christmas this had turned out to be! Abbie thought contentedly.

The Rock was still enveloped in fog the next morning, but inside the house Christmas Day was bright for the Burgesses. The girls began unwrapping gifts early. The mysterious hammering sounds that had come from their father's workshop for so many weeks had produced doll cradles for the younger girls, a small box in which Lydia could keep her button and pressed-flower collections, and a large chest for Abbie.

During the quiet hours she'd spent in her room—hours that worried Abbie so—Mrs. Burgess had been crocheting a bedspread for Abbie's hope chest. "I started it a year ago, Abigail. It was high time I finished it."

On his last trip to the mainland, Mr. Burgess had bought some gifts. There were water colors for Lydia, a new diary for Abbie, and games and books for Esther and Mahala.

Everyone fancied Lydia's drawings. She'd sketched her father leaning over the dory; Abbie sitting by the sea; and Esther and Mahala playing outside with their dolls. She'd made a charcoal sketch of her mother in her rocker, mending by the lamplight.

"Your father will frame them," her mother promised, "and hang them in our rooms."

Mahala and Esther hovered about as their homemade presents were opened by the other family members. They had chosen their prettiest moon shell for their mother. Some dried seaweed had been fashioned into a holder for their father's pipes, and a string of shells formed a necklace for Lydia.

But the gifts that brought the most chuckles were the Indian headdresses Abbie had made for Esther and Mahala out of gull feathers glued onto bands of ribbon. Abbie then gave out the red mittens she'd made for her sisters and the warm brown shawl she'd knitted for her mother. She hesitated over the pair of gloves she'd worked on for her father, for she wanted Caleb to have something. Later, she could knit another pair for her father to match the muffler she had for him.

"If we'd known you were going to be our guest for Christmas," she said now to Caleb, "we'd have had more presents for you under the tree. But all our best wishes are wrapped up in one gift."

Caleb smiled sheepishly. "I'll never forget your kindness,"

he told them all as he opened the package and admired the thickness of the gloves. "These are the finest I've ever owned."

Benjy was pleased with his gloves, too. "I really needed these, Sis."

At last, Mahala and Esther presented Abbie with their gift for her. It was part of a page torn from a Bible. "Mahala and I found it washed up on the shore," Esther explained. "Father read it to us, then he marked one of the lines for us. It's from Matthew."

Abbie read aloud the words that had been underlined: " 'Let your light so shine before men . . .' " She smiled fondly at her sisters. "It warms my heart to have this. I'll paste it inside my diary and treasure it always."

Mr. Burgess and Benjy extinguished and cleaned the lamps that morning. Abbie spent the morning in the kitchen helping prepare the Christmas dinner. With two unexpected guests, they expanded the menu. The younger girls peeled, chopped, and sampled, while tantalizing smells filled the house.

By three o'clock, the turkey was roasted to perfection. They sat down to eat, including Caleb in their circle of joined hands. The prayer Mr. Burgess offered was one of his most impressive, Abbie thought. He expressed humble gratitude for the safe journey of the young men to the lighthouse, and he sought the Lord's care for them on their return trip to their ships.

That afternoon, Benjy led Caleb about, showing him the workings of the lighthouse station. Abbie took him to the towers with her when she lighted the lamps at sunset.

During the evening, as they sat in front of the fire, Caleb

said, "Being here with you people—well, it's cheered me no end. Until you've been out at sea, tossing about in a storm or lost in a fog—certain you'll never touch land again—you'll never rightly know how good it feels suddenly to see a light in the darkness or to hear the sound of a bell."

His words left them all silent. Abbie knew their work was important, but it was satisfying to hear a seaman, a shipwrecked seaman, tell them so.

Later, when she said a last good night to the girls, Abbie was startled to have Mahala raise up from beneath the bedcovers and whisper, "Abbie, are you going to marry Caleb?"

"Mahala, where did you ever get such a notion?"

"Don't you recollect? Benjy said you'd probably marry a shipwrecked sailor. You like Caleb, and I suspect he likes you. Esther and I think he's quite handsome, and he could live right here at the lighthouse with us."

If Abbie hadn't been so weary, she'd have giggled. "Mahala, you go to sleep! Tomorrow, I'll have to explain to you why young ladies don't speculate about such things."

Down under her own quilts at last, Abbie smiled to herself.

The fog lifted during the night, and the Rock lay sharply defined in the morning light. Benjy and Caleb spent the day in the boathouse repairing the damages to Caleb's dory.

At dawn the next day, Benjy and his father helped Caleb to launch his boat. Abbie got breakfast for them, and then fixed a basket of food for Caleb to take along. She stood on the ledge and watched him put out to sea. She waved good-by until he disappeared from sight.

"I'll never forget this holiday," he'd said just before he left, "nor will I ever forget you, Abbie Burgess. Whenever I see a lighthouse, I'll remember the Burgesses, and the young girl who climbs the towers every evening to light the lamps."

He had pressed her hand gently. She was glad Mahala and Esther had not witnessed the scene, for they'd never have stopped planning a wedding for her. It would be hard to convince them that she liked Caleb only in the same way she liked Benjy.

CHAPTER XIII

A Visit with Prissy

It was a long winter, but as March passed, signs of spring were all about. A year older now, Abbie handled heavier chores with confidence. On balmy days, she helped her father scrape and whitewash the rain barrels and repair the damage to the sheds caused by the heavy snows and rains.

With a year of growth, her sisters complained less and took on more of the cooking and ironing, leaving Abbie time to work with her father.

In May, when the lobstering season began, the two of them went out in the dory every day to set the traps and haul in the catch. One morning while they were out lobstering, Benjy sailed up to the Rock, surprising them all, for they'd heard from him only a few times since his Christmas visit.

The younger girls followed him about, admiring his manly swagger, more exaggerated now, and his tales of life at sea. Mrs. Burgess mended his clothes and trimmed his hair.

"Now that you've had a taste of the sea," Mr. Burgess said,

concerned about Benjy's plans for the future, "I reckon you appreciate what we have here, Son."

"That's all I've had, Father," Benjy replied, "just a taste. But it was enough to know the sea is in my blood."

After another day with his family, Benjy left to rejoin his ship.

Busy as she was with her father, Abbie seldom had time for outings with her sisters, and they were no longer content with the simple pleasures the Rock offered. It was Lydia who first talked of visiting Rockland. Mrs. Haskell had invited her to spend several days with her, so when Mr. Burgess cast off with a catch of lobsters one bright June morning, Lydia went with him.

Soon after, Esther and Mahala begged to go, and since Mrs. Haskell was willing, the next time Lydia went, the younger girls went along.

Lydia tried to persuade Abbie to visit Rockland. "You won't believe your eyes! All the new buildings and stores— and so many young ladies sashaying around just like Prissy."

"I'm glad you enjoyed it," Abbie said. "But if I went to Rockland with Father, who would tend the lights?"

"Why, you could go on the supply boat at the end of the lobstering—before the very cold weather sets in."

That was months away, and Abbie didn't like to plan so far ahead. Anyhow, how could a visit to Rockland be as satisfying as keeping the lighthouse?

Mr. Burgess brought back enticing news with every trip. Rockland was an incorporated town now. On July 1, their first council meeting had been held and Knott Crockett was elected mayor. In November, the town would have its first public water-supply system.

Shipbuilding, especially for the clipper trade, was at a peak. By next year, her father had heard, one-third of all the ships built in the nation would be constructed in Maine. And Rockland was one of the most important shipbuilding towns.

Prissy's letters were just as colorful. In late July, she wrote: "This has been a busy summer, with so many fancy parties. Rockland has a new fire engine, the State of Maine #3, and they've even built an engine house for it. On the Fourth of July, there was a grand ball at the Georges Hotel. The firemen wore red jackets and white trousers. I wore a new yellow dress and danced with three of the handsomest firemen there.

"Then, right in the middle of the ball, the fire alarm sounded. The men dashed out in their uniforms, climbed aboard the engine, and went clanging down the street. The Carr building was on fire. It was saved, but the men's uniforms were all ruined. Now Papa will have to order new ones for them from New York."

At times, Abbie longed to see Rockland, to hear the church bells tolling again, to browse in the Ladies' Library, to visit Mr. Pratt's store. But it was the waterfront that beckoned her most. Her father's description of some of the latest clipper ships fairly dazzled her. Were they really so enormous?

Lobstering season had no sooner ended than winter began to batter the Rock with snow and ice. The supply boat missed its December trip, so they celebrated Christmas in January, when the cutter finally brought their supplies and a tree.

The younger girls endured the long afternoons with more patience that second winter. Their mother taught them how to knit, crochet, and sew a few simple garments, and Mr. Burgess enlarged their studies to include history and politics. Benjy's letters grew further apart, and Abbie was obliged to remind her mother often that they would have to trust God that all was well with him.

Abbie always read Prissy's letters aloud, knowing how they amused her mother. In June of the following year—1855—there was one telling about another new fire engine. "It's called Eureka #4," Prissy wrote. "Eureka means 'I have found it!' It's quite a popular word. Everyone uses it. Papa says he hopes he never has to hear it again.

"They held a grand parade with the Rockland guards and a brass band. Thirty-one young ladies representing various states rode in a 'floral-car'—a wagon hitched together and draped with flowers. I was one of the girls from Maine.

"We went to Beach Woods Grove for a picnic and a band concert. After that, they shot off fireworks. During the display, it began to rain. Everyone dashed to their carriages and wagons, and there I sat—my lovely white gown ruined. Why do my good times always end in disaster?

"Another clipper ship will be launched week after next. Do come for a visit, so we can see the launching together. I'll show you a grand time, Abbie."

Abbie folded the letter slowly.

"You really should go, Abigail," her mother urged. "It's different for me. That boat trip would tire me out so I wouldn't enjoy myself. But you should have some good times, child, while you're young. Those lamps are rightly your father's work."

Abbie talked it over with her father, and he made the

necessary arrangements. He would postpone the lobstering until she returned.

The night before her departure, Abbie packed her two best dresses and her underthings in a valise. Just before daylight her father woke her. After she dressed and had breakfast, she went down to the landing with him to await the cutter. It had stopped for the night at one of the neighboring islands, and the captain had agreed to pick her up on the way back to Rockland.

Looking down at her simple calico dress and high-topped leather shoes, Abbie thought of Prissy's fancy pink dress and parasol the day she came to the Rock. It made her feel as plain as the rock beneath her feet.

After the cutter started on its course to the mainland, Abbie glanced back at the Rock. Seeing it from afar, she wondered what others felt when they caught sight of the house and towers. Did they think of it as just another landmark to guide them on their journey? Or were they curious about the people who lived on that lonely Rock, who tended those lights?

The sail to Rockland seemed twice as long as their trip out to Matinicus Rock on that first day. As the cutter glided into the harbor at last, Abbie's gaze became fixed on the giant clipper ship in the shipyard across the harbor. It waited there, ready for the launching ceremony.

Prissy was standing on the wharf, with a parasol shading her face.

"Abbie, you've grown so!" she exclaimed, smelling of perfume, as she kissed Abbie's cheek. Abbie blushed as Prissy measured her waistline with her eyes, and studied the texture of her skin. "And you're so *brown*. I knew you'd stay out in that awful sun too much. Wait'll I dress you up proper. You'll steal away all my beaus."

Abbie felt uncomfortable with Prissy's talk about beaus and fancy clothes. She'd come to visit, to have long chats and share secrets the way they had before. Had two years changed all that? Yet, as she listened to Prissy ramble on about her social life, and the winter wardrobe her mother had ordered for her, Abbie knew that Prissy hadn't changed. She'd just widened her private world to include Boston and New York.

"Papa often takes me to Boston with him," Prissy explained. "Last time we had dinner in a fancy restaurant, and I wore my scarlet velvet gown and had my hair up in curls. One of Papa's friends offered me a glass of wine. Papa wouldn't let me have any, of course, but it was thrilling to be taken for an older woman."

Abbie wished, for a moment, that she was back on the Rock where everything was familiar, where she knew what to do and what was expected of her.

"There I go," Prissy said, "rattling on again!" She touched Abbie's hand. "I'm giving a small party tonight, and you're the guest of honor. Some of my classmates will be there. They still remember you. They don't believe a girl your age could be happy living on a lighthouse station, and they'll try to trick you into saying so. If you didn't bring along a party dress, I'd be pleasured to lend you one of mine."

Dressing for the party, Abbie felt entirely helpless. Prissy insisted that she wear a corset, and Abbie slipped into it reluctantly. Prissy laced it up, all the while reminding her how unfeminine it was to have a thick waistline. As Prissy fastened the last hook, Abbie gasped, "I can't breathe! Prissy, my eyes will be bulging out of my head!"

Prissy paid her no heed, saying only, "Ladies don't use such vulgar expressions." She brought out a dress of blue silk, slipped it over Abbie's head, and hooked it up the back. She sat Abbie down in front of her dressing table, brushed her hair, and then pinned it up. After that, she dusted her face and shoulders with powder, dabbed her with perfume, and tucked a white flower behind her ear. Lastly, she brought out a pair of blue satin slippers.

"Now," she exclaimed, "wait 'til our friends see *you!* Lighthouse Keeper's daughter—indeed!"

Abbie might have believed she was staring at a stranger's reflection were it not for the corset squeezing the breath out of her, the shoes pinching her feet, and hair that threatened to slip from its mooring at any moment.

She followed Prissy into the parlor uneasily, trying to remember all the ladylike things she'd been coached to say. She was startled to see how much taller and older her friends were, especially the boys in their fancy coats. The girls, gowned in velvets and silks, were as dignified as Prissy. They were all quite curious about Abbie's life on the Rock.

She nibbled little cakes, sipped pink punch, and answered questions. Thad Beaumont and Charles Payson knew a great deal about the lighthouse service. They talked about the times they'd sailed past Matinicus Rock, and the day they'd tried to land there and nearly smashed their dory.

Prissy tried to steer the conversation back to Rockland, but when one of the boys pointedly asked Abbie if she really lighted those lamps by herself, and she admitted it was so, even the girls were intrigued. Abbie was overjoyed to describe the lighthouse work. Yet, except for Thad and Charles, she couldn't imagine any of them being willing to stay on the Rock for very long.

It was nearly midnight when the guests left, and the girls tiptoed to Prissy's bedroom. Abbie had never seen a sight so inviting as Prissy's plump bed with its soft white linens. Shedding the binding corset at last, she slipped into her nightgown and sank down against the pillows.

Abbie closed her eyes, eager to sleep, but Prissy flitted about the room, pleased about the impression Abbie had made on the young men.

"Why, you had all the attention, Abbie. And Jed Tobias—well, you really charmed *him*." She went on about her plans for the next day. She intended to show Abbie a good time, but she was still set on making her look fashionable. "Tomorrow," she said, "we'll try to lighten your tan some. Lemon juice should do it."

Abbie awoke to a strange sensation—sunshine warming her face. She raised up suddenly, remembering the lamps. *I forgot to blow them out!* Her eyes fell on the pink painted walls of Prissy's room and her memory came back, and with it a rush of sadness that she was so far away from the Rock.

Prissy's cook served the girls toast, marmalade, and hot tea for breakfast. Abbie was sure she'd faint from hunger before dinner, but she forgot her appetite once Prissy began to discuss the launching.

"Launching days are quite a holiday in Rockland now," she said. "Shops close, a band plays, and they even sell refreshments."

Abbie's enthusiasm increased until she learned that Prissy expected her to wear a corset and fancy dress again. "I can't spend a whole day rigged out like that, Prissy. I just *can't!*"

"But everyone will be there, Abbie. Please, dress up this morning, and you can traipse around in comfort the rest of the day."

Mr. Pratt sent his carriage around for them shortly before the ceremony. Sitting beside Prissy in the open carriage, with a parasol tilted over her head, Abbie was glad she'd yielded to Prissy's pleas. She wished her mother and sisters could see how grand she looked riding through Rockland this way.

At the shipyard, the whole area was jammed with townspeople, carriages, and horses. Children romped about, and dogs barked wildly. The driver parked their carriage at a spot that gave them a good view of the ceremony.

A platform, trimmed with red, white, and blue paper streamers, had been erected for the occasion, and officials were gathering there. Behind the stand was the vessel itself, the sun reflecting off her sleek gray bulk. The masts and sails would be added after the ship was afloat.

"Isn't she a regal sight!" Prissy exclaimed. "Papa went aboard and counted fourteen staterooms, all finished in mahogany and black walnut and trimmed in gilt. It'll take a hundred men to sail her."

One of the officials stood up, and the crowd fell silent. Heads bowed as he began to ask the Almighty for protection for the clipper and its crew, freedom to roam the seas, and the ability to strengthen ties between the countries where the vessel would trade.

Prissy whispered, "Years ago, they broke a bottle of rum over the bow, then passed barrels of rum among the crowd.

But now they have this religious ceremony and christen the ship with water."

Abbie nodded, amused at Prissy, who'd forgotten that Abbie had seen a few launchings when she lived in Rockland. But this one was more impressive than any she'd attended.

Presently, another man stepped forward and declared, "I christen thee, *Young Mechanic!*" He swung a bottle, and its crash against the clipper's bow brought applause from the crowd. Then a cannon boomed, and the ship slipped slowly down the greased ways and moved out into the harbor, its gilt figurehead glistening in the sun.

"There, now," Prissy exclaimed, "it's launched! And one of these days it will start on its maiden voyage." She directed the driver to take them through the business district on the way home, so she could point out the new sights in Rockland.

Abbie was properly impressed with the big hotel and other buildings she hadn't seen before. But the houses were still close, even closer than she remembered, and the lime smoke choked her after the fresh air of the Rock.

She'd never dined so elegantly as she did at supper that evening. The Pratts' dining room boasted a carpet all the way from Persia, chairs covered with needlepoint, and a glittering crystal chandelier.

Mrs. Pratt made polite inquiries about the health of Abbie's mother and sisters. She remarked about the bravery of the Burgesses, and said how thankful people were that such a fine family had become guardians of the coast.

Mr. Pratt predicted a depression ahead for Rockland, and asked Abbie to pass his views along to her father. Already, shipbuilding was declining and work was getting scarce.

Prissy won permission to attend a picnic which their

friends were giving the next day. When they left the house to go to the picnic, they took along a large, scarlet umbrella to shelter them from the sun, and wore long gloves to keep their arms from getting tanned.

Abbie had set her mind on enjoying herself, but it was all so strange. The young people mentioned places and things that were foreign to her. When Jed Tobias invited her to go rowing with him, she quickly accepted, certain she would feel at home once she was out on the water. But she hadn't counted on Jed's lack of seamanship. No sooner were they afloat than he stood up in the rowboat, rocking it from side to side.

"Jed," Abbie begged, "please sit down before we capsize."

"Why, Abbie," he taunted, "you couldn't be afraid of a little water—not you, a lighthouse keeper's daughter."

With that, the boat turned over, and they were both in the water. Jed shoved the boat toward Abbie. "Hold on," he said, "I'll get you ashore."

Their plight had been noticed by their friends, and soon Thad and Charles came to their rescue.

"I'm sorry, truly I am," Prissy apologized as she rubbed Abbie's hair dry with a towel. "I didn't count on Jed being such a show-off. Stop shivering so! The sun will warm you through, and after we eat, we'll go home."

The sun did warm her, and the food was tasty, but Abbie's thoughts dwelled on tomorrow when she could board the cutter and sail for home. As fond as she was of Prissy, she could not take to Prissy's ways or fit into her kind of life.

Just before they parted at the wharf, Prissy took her hand. "We're as different as winter and summer, Abbie, but even so, it lifts my spirits to be with you."

Abbie felt tearful as she said good-by, but only because she was uncertain how long it might be before she saw Prissy and Rockland again. The Rock was her real place, though—where she rightly belonged. She'd never been as sure of it as she was now.

CHAPTER XIV

Winter of the Tempests

THE SUPPLY BOAT missed its September call. As long as the lobster season lasted, Mr. Burgess picked up needed provisions whenever he hauled the catch to the mainland. But when the cutter still hadn't arrived by the end of October, he told his family: "I may be obliged to go after the rations myself. More'n likely they'll have to skip us in December, and we can't fare the winter without more supplies. Meanwhile, it's best we be sparing in our use of everything."

Snow fell several times before the week was out and wind and waves lashed the Rock with great force. Abbie was careful not to waste food or spill any oil, and her father kept a close eye on the barometer.

During the first week of November it snowed so heavily that Mr. Burgess decided to move the hen coop to higher ground. Abbie went out with him to help and to feed the hens.

"Are we in for a bad winter, Father?"

"I'm afraid so, Daughter. That's all that keeps me from

striking out for the mainland today. I daren't leave until the weather clears some."

Abbie brushed snow off a boulder, sat down upon it, and held one of the hens in her lap. "Father, you promised that if a bad storm was brewing, you'd move Mother into the parlor. I've wondered how we could do that without upsetting her. But now that we must save fuel, she'll believe we're moving her so she'll be closer to the warm kitchen. If you've a mind, you could tell her so tonight."

Her father was silent for a moment. "You're a smart one, Daughter. I hadn't thought of that excuse."

At supper, Mr. Burgess explained to his wife that he favored moving their bedroom from the wooden chamber into the parlor.

"The temperature's dropping fast," he went on. "It'll be more'n ten below tonight, I calculate. If we all stay close to the kitchen, we'll be warm."

Mrs. Burgess looked grave. "I know we're in for a hard winter, Sam, and I don't mind changing my bedroom. But I think you should set out for the mainland. We've got to have food and other supplies."

"I'll go tomorrow, Thankful—most likely."

That evening, Abbie's father hauled the bedroom furniture into the parlor, and soon the parlor resembled a gracious sitting room.

"Oh, Mother," Abbie exclaimed, as she glanced about, "we should have put you in here that first day. It's bigger, the view is lovely, and we seldom use this room."

Her mother drew her closer. "Abigail, I'm not fooled. Your father suspects a storm and fears the wooden section will be washed away. I've felt it in my bones lately. Something terrible's ahead for us!"

"Mother!" Abbie sank down beside her on the bed. "Please don't think such things. It'll only make you ill. Father's trying to conserve our fuel—that's all."

There was sleet the next morning, so Mr. Burgess had to postpone his trip. Abbie helped him scrape ice off the tower windows and keep the walks shoveled clear.

She was grateful that her mother felt strong enough to spend the afternoons supervising the girls. While she sat there in front of the fire, working on a quilt for Abbie's hope chest, she urged the younger girls to keep busy at the pastimes they enjoyed.

On her eleventh birthday that autumn, Mahala had inherited Lydia's button chest with its fascinating contents. Esther, now twelve, had taken Abbie's place as her mother's baking assistant. She went through her mother's recipes and tried out the ones that sounded most delicious. Her latest specialty was making preserves.

Now a lady of fourteen, Lydia had turned her artistic talent to needlework. Her mother patiently taught her tatting, knitting, and fine embroidery work, and Lydia made her own patterns.

Though they were constantly occupied, the girls complained no end about the inconvenience the cutter's delay was causing them. There were no letters from Benjy or their friends, no newspapers, and no new buttons from Mrs. Haskell.

They fretted most about the food. One evening, Lydia burst out, "I wouldn't mind the salt pork and beans, even smoked fish—if it weren't for Thanksgiving. But all my Rockland friends will have plump turkeys, cranberries, and mince pie."

"That'll be enough, Lydia," Mr. Burgess scolded. "We have plenty of good food. It needn't be fancy to be nourishing."

Despite their hopes, Thanksgiving came and there was no turkey, nor did their quarterly rations arrive. With the ocean so rough, none of them expected a boat to risk a landing at the Rock.

On Thanksgiving morning, Mr. Burgess loaded the gun he kept locked away and shot a large sea bird for their dinner. Abbie helped to clean and roast it, but she didn't fancy its strange flavor or tough meat. Her mother and sisters, however, were pleased to have such a change in their diet.

Several times in early December, Mr. Burgess got the dory ready for the trip, but he couldn't leave. One morning, he put it down the ways, but the tide had risen so high that the breakers slapped the boat angrily against the ledge.

"You can't go!" Abbie shouted above the thundering waves. "You'd never make it to land!" Her father nodded in agreement.

While they were sitting at dinner that day, a breaker splashed over the ledge of the Rock, washed in several yards, then rolled back to sea. Esther and Mahala began to cry, afraid the ocean would wash clear up to the house.

"Now, girls," their father said, "you've seen spray dash over the Rock every winter now and not come any farther. But all the same, we must take precautions." He assigned each one a duty, and they hustled about as if their lives depended on their promptness.

The little ones hauled in more wood from the shed. Abbie and Lydia latched the wooden shutters on the windows. Mr. Burgess hurried outside, tied everything down, and closed the doors and windows of the sheds.

Abbie kept a close watch on the ocean. The breakers were coming nearer to the house. The next one would probably wash under the fog bell. She tried not to dwell on the entries in the old logs—especially the one of January 1839, when the Keeper and his family spent the night on the storm-tossed sea.

By evening, the wind was of gale force. During the nightly Bible reading, the roaring became more intense. Suddenly, there was the unmistakable sound of ocean spray striking the windows of the chamber behind the tower. Abbie clearly read her father's glance; they had moved her mother just in time.

It was a strain for Mr. Burgess to talk loud enough for them to hear, so he kept his own message brief. "We can't still the storm, as Jesus did in the Bible reading, but we can have faith that God will watch over us and this lighthouse tonight. Now, off to bed, and sleep in peace."

While her sisters trooped upstairs, Abbie asked her father, "Should I help you watch the lamps, Father? You can't stay up all night."

"No, Daughter. You save your strength; it may be needed more later."

Upstairs, she found Esther and Mahala sobbing with fright, and Lydia fuming at both of them. Abbie hugged them close until they fell asleep, then she slipped into her own bed in the next room.

The storm wore itself out within the week, but it was still

too rough for sailing, so Christmas came without the sight of a boat.

Mr. Burgess collected some wooden slats, built a framework in the shape of a pine tree, and draped it with lengths of seaweed. On Christmas Eve, after the girls were in bed, he set the tree up in the kitchen. Abbie tacked a starfish on top, and strung leftover decorations around the seaweed "branches." She piled their homemade gifts under the tree.

Early Christmas morning, Mr. Burgess stamped into the kitchen, his dark eyes aglow. He held up a large codfish that was speared on a stick. Its tail was still flapping.

"The Lord does provide! It was surely Providence that led me down to the shore this morning. Look what I found washed up there."

At dinner, Mr. Burgess told the children that in those parts, such a catch in the dead of winter was called a "Marblehead turkey."

Esther beamed at this. "Now, we're having turkey for Christmas dinner after all."

The codfish meat was tender and delicious, as grand as any turkey, and there was enough for all to stuff themselves. It was a joyous day, despite their predicament.

Along toward evening, Abbie noticed a pinched look about her mother's face, and a little later, she found her in her parlor bedroom, lying under a quilt.

"Mother, what's wrong?"

"I've felt poorly all day, Abigail. But if I let on to your father, he won't leave. And he's obliged to get those supplies."

Abbie gave her some tonic, assuring her that the situation

was far from serious. "We've got enough provisions to last a month or so, and the weather's bound to break soon."

But even as she talked, snow was drifting down outside, and it was followed by sleet. The trip had to be postponed once more.

Mr. Burgess wasn't unduly concerned about his wife's spell of illness. She had no fever or pain, and as long as her tonic lasted, she would be all right. Abbie agreed with him that Mother had just worn herself down with worry and that she'd surely improve once he made the trip. But he couldn't hide his concern about the weather.

If it hadn't been so serious, Abbie might have made a game of wondering which would appear first—a calm sea or the bottom of the flour barrel. She didn't dare calculate how many meals the balance would make, for she felt that would be doubting God's care for them.

The year 1856 arrived with fresh sleet and driving snow, and Abbie and her father were kept continually busy clearing walks and tower windows. During the second week of January, the sleet slackened, and then one day the snow stopped.

On the night of January 18, Mr. Burgess told his family, "The sea's calm now, and the barometer's steady. Tomorrow, I'll set sail for Rockland."

The next morning, he hoisted the flag for the first time in many weeks. When he came in, he said, "Must be the start of the January thaw. I reckon I'll have a good sail."

After breakfast, he went to his wife's room and kissed her good-by. "Now, Thankful, don't you fret while I'm gone. I'll be back in two days, three at the most, loaded down with good things."

Abbie bundled up warmly and went to the dory with her father. At the landing, she helped him slide the dory down the ways. The sea was as calm as on a summer day.

Her father held her close. "Abigail, I know I can depend on you to keep the lights burning."

Abbie tightened his muffler around his neck and buttoned the top of his heavy coat. "You know I will, Father," she said. "It's my duty."

She stood on the ledge above and watched as the dory rose and fell softly on the waves. She waited until the sail was a white speck in the distance; then she started back to the house.

In the first tower, she went about her duties. Now and then, she peered through the telescope for one more glimpse of the *Provider*. After she'd taken care of things in the second tower, she joined her sisters in the kitchen. They were eating the gruel and biscuits she'd left on the stove.

"Is Father really on his way to Rockland?" Mahala asked.

When Abbie told them that he was well on the way, they all shouted with joy.

CHAPTER XV

The Great Storm

THE GIRLS STAMPED about in their snowshoes for over an hour, pelting one another with snowballs and playing with the hens. It was good to hear them laughing again, Abbie thought, as she finished her morning chores.

While they were eating dinner, the kitchen became so dark that Abbie got up to light the lamp. As she did so, a gust of wind whined down the chimney, followed by a blast that set the shutters slamming furiously against the house.

She ran to the window. The clear sky had deepened to an ominous dark gray. Gulls screamed wildly as if bewitched by the wind. From the way the flag on the pole was blowing, she knew the wind had veered to the northeast.

Esther and Mahala began to cry, and Mrs. Burgess called out from the parlor, "Abigail, your father's caught in this storm!"

"Now, Mother, he's halfway to the mainland by now. And it may be just a gale that'll blow right out to sea."

Esther and Mahala rushed in to them. "What'll we do, Abbie?" Esther asked worriedly.

"We'll do exactly what Father would if he were here. We'll batten things down." She directed Lydia and Esther to latch all the shutters, and Mahala was sent to bring in the flag.

Abbie closed up the sheds and moved the hen coop to a more protected spot. After all was done, her sisters sat around the fire, complaining about being alone on the Rock without their father or Benjy.

"Now Father can't bring back the supplies until the storm's over," Lydia whined. "And that might be several days!"

"We won't dwell on that," Abbie told her. "We'll take each day as it comes. I'd best light the lamps early today. It's so dark."

With each hour, the wind grew more frenzied, until it was battering the Rock unmercifully. Huge breakers flung themselves at the ledges.

Abbie lost count of the hours she spent minding the lamps. In between her vigil, she kept her loved ones warm and fed, and calmed their fears. She watered down her mother's tonic as much as she dared, wishing she could spoon courage into her as easily as she did the tonic. Yet, she marveled at her mother's composure, in view of their serious situation.

At night, Mahala slept with Mrs. Burgess, and Lydia and Esther spread pallets by the fireside. Abbie, exhausted from her labors, was glad to have the comfort of the couch.

For a week, there was no relief from the hurricane winds. It was as though the elements had gone mad and were venting all their fury upon the Rock. On the eighth morning,

Abbie was awakened by a loud boom. She sat up, every nerve taut. A breaker had slammed against the house!

She hurried up to the tower and was relieved to find the lamps still glowing. The sky was so dark, she let the lamps burn on, though the oil was scarce. In the light the towers cast, she could see gray billows heaving offshore. Each one rose higher than the one before it, and splashed farther upon the Rock.

When Abbie returned to the kitchen, she found Lydia struggling to help Esther make a batch of griddle cakes. Mahala was using towels to mop up water from a leak under the kitchen door. They all turned to Abbie with frightened faces.

"It's worse," Lydia said, her lips quivering.

Mahala shouted, "Are we going to be washed away?"

"Not likely." Abbie tried to smile. "After we eat, things won't seem so gloomy."

The morning passed swiftly and without incident, but just as they began to eat dinner, a breaker crashed on the roof with the boom of a cannon. They clung to each other in terror, as if waiting for the end. Time passed, and there was only a terrible, deafening roar.

When the furor quieted some, Abbie sprang to her feet. "Mother, the coop is bound to be flooded. I must get my hens before they drown——"

Her mother grabbed her dress. "Abigail, you daren't go outside! You'll be swept right out to sea!"

"But I can't bear to part with my hens. If I go before another breaker comes—there's a chance."

She grabbed a basket, and when the sea fell back a little,

she ran down the steps. The water came up to her knees, but she pushed on until she came to the coop. She opened the door and the hens tumbled out. She scooped two into the basket, and the others flapped about frantically. Two white feathery forms were sinking into the water, but she pulled them out and dropped them into the basket. She couldn't find the fifth hen. There was no time left to search, for another breaker was rumbling toward her.

Mahala opened the back door, and Abbie dashed inside. "Oh, look!" Mahala exclaimed. "Look there! The worst sea is coming!"

A gigantic billow, about thirty feet in height, was lunging toward the Rock.

"*Close the door!*" Abbie yelled.

Mahala screamed and shut the door. Abbie flung the basket down, the hens scattering, and hurried to the sideboard near the door.

"Help me bar the door!" she cried, pushing against the weight of it. Her sisters came and pitted their strength with hers, and the chest slid in front of the door just as the breaker struck. The house trembled from the impact. They leaned limply against the sideboard, certain this was the final blow.

After a moment, when it appeared the house had survived, Mrs. Burgess burst into sobs. The younger girls ran to her, while Lydia took pity on the squawking hens and gathered them into her lap. Suddenly, she shrieked, "Where's Patience? Abbie—what happened to Patience?"

Abbie shook her head sadly. "I—I couldn't find her. The water was so deep." She was as heartsick over the loss as the girls, but she decided to let them cry, for it would relieve the strain. Right now, she had to check to see what damage had been done. Entering the tower, she stepped into a pool of water. She held her breath and quickly opened the door leading to the wooden chamber.

"Sakes' alive!" she gasped. The space where the room had been was an abyss of swirling water. Only the stone foundation stood. She shut the door and leaned against it as horror filled her mind. Her mother might have been in that room!

She took stock of the situation. The ocean had already washed away the wooden section of the house, and if the storm got any worse, the house itself might not stand. The towers, she decided, were their only chance.

In the kitchen, she removed her wet boots, put on dry shoes, and hung all her wet clothing near the fire to dry. She bided her time in telling the others about the plans that were forming in her mind.

As they were finishing their evening meal, she said, "Mother, we'd best move into the tower until the storm's over. The lamp room would be right comfortable."

"The tower!" Lydia interrupted. "It smells horrid in there!"

"We'd freeze," Esther put in.

Mrs. Burgess shook her head. "Abigail, I won't let anyone sleep up there."

"The lamps give a lot of heat," Abbie pointed out.

"But there's no sense going up there, Abigail."

Abbie sighed. "Then I'm obliged to tell you," she said, struggling to keep her voice steady. "The—the wooden chamber was washed away this morning. The timbers are probably strewn about Penobscot Bay right now. I figure the towers are stronger than the house. We'll be safer there."

Lydia continued to protest, and Abbie's mother insisted

she couldn't endure the climb up the tower stairs. Abbie argued with them until she was hoarse.

She put soap stones on top of the stove to heat, to help keep their feet warm. She collected the bedding and a basket of food, and when all was ready, she led the two younger girls up to the tower off the kitchen. When she had them settled comfortably in the lamp room, she went back down and asked her mother once more.

"No, Abigail," she replied, "I'll stay here and keep the fire going. Lydia can stay with me."

Abbie went back to the tower, knowing that if things worsened, they'd come up to the lamp room. When she entered, with a Betty lamp in one hand and the family Bible in the other, Mahala looked at her strangely. "What did you bring the Bible for?"

"So I can read it," she said. "Father reads the Bible every night, doesn't he?"

The lamp room, though ten feet in diameter, was small compared to the kitchen, so Abbie was able to speak in a more normal tone. She turned to the passages in the seventh chapter of Matthew where Jesus spoke about the house built upon a rock. She read it with conviction, then explained to her sisters that the rock to which the Master referred was the rock of faith.

"We must have faith that the house will survive and that Father will return safely."

Sometime after they were finally asleep, Abbie went to the shelf where the lamps were burning and opened the log book. It was just after midnight. She dipped a pen into the ink well and made this entry: "January 27, 1856. A nor'easter blowing in. We're prepared for the worst."

She donned the oilskins and boots she'd brought up to the tower. After another breaker passed overhead, she quickly went out on the catwalk to scrape the windows before the next breaker struck.

She stepped into a pit of blackness that was terrifying. The wind screamed and buffeted her against the tower, and needles of ice pricked her cheeks. The ocean lapped viciously below the tower, as though it were a monster eager to swallow the house and towers. Knowing that her next step might be into eternity, she prayed.

With the below-zero temperatures, the ocean spray froze instantly on the glass panes, yet there was only a thin layer of ice on each window. The heat from the lamps inside, she decided, kept the windows slightly warm. The warning grumble of another breaker sent her back inside.

On the next try, she finished scraping all the windows. She rested a spell, then began the journey to the other tower. It seemed peculiar not to hear her own footsteps, for in good weather, her feet fairly boomed in the granite tower. But tonight, it was as though she walked on velvet.

She went on through the house, passing her mother, who was sleeping on the couch, and Lydia stretched on a pallet nearby. She climbed up to the second tower. Out on the second catwalk, she clung to the railing, not daring to look down at the swirling water below. She began to sing a hymn and its words gave her the courage to complete her task.

Back in the first tower, she snuggled close to her sleeping sisters and closed her eyes. She wondered drowsily if Mr. Pratt had put her father up for the night, and she hoped Benjy was in calmer waters. Thinking of Benjy, she couldn't help wondering how things might have worked out if he'd been here. Would he now be tending the lamps? Or would he have gone to the mainland for the supplies? It had been two years since they'd laid eyes on him. He was man-grown, for sure.

She dozed only, waking at intervals to check the lamps; then she'd drop off again. All of a sudden, she felt someone shaking her. She sat up and saw Lydia, holding the lamp from the kitchen table. Her mouth was moving, but no sound came out.

This must be what it's like to be deaf, Abbie thought giddily as she realized the storm had worsened. Lydia screamed into her ear. "The kitchen's flooding, Abbie! Mother's trying to save the rug. You must come!"

Abbie got to her feet, stiff and cold, and followed Lydia into the kitchen. She found their mother on her hands and knees, mopping at the braided rug, while salt water poured over it in a continuous stream.

Abbie pulled her mother up and sat her on the couch. "You're too weak to do that, Mother. The rug isn't ruined. It'll dry out. Come—you and Lydia *must* go to the tower with me. It's dry and warmer up there."

Putting her mother's arm across her shoulders, Abbie supported her weight as they mounted the stairs. No heavy work she'd done for her father compared to the exertion of that climb. With her last bit of energy, she arranged the bedding.

"Mercy," her mother moaned. "I wish your father was here. I'm too sick to help you, and you don't have the strength——"

Abbie patted her shoulder. "God will give me the strength to do my duty, Mother. You sleep now."

"It's a good thing you've got such faith, Abigail. We'll all be needing it before this is over."

Abbie slept for a little while, then awoke to attend to the lamps. Wrapped in the oilskins, she went down to the kitchen. The parlor was flooded now, but she walked through it. The lamps in the second tower flickered as she entered, but blazed right up again.

The wind had an eerie, high-pitched whine, as Abbie stepped out on the catwalk, and the water still churned below. She chipped at the icy windows until her hands began to ache despite her thick gloves.

At the first streak of dawn, she snuffed out the lamps, eager to save the precious oil. The ocean's fury was still blasting the Rock, but it was easier to bear in daylight, Abbie discovered.

She managed to build a fire in the stove and put on a pot of cornmeal mush. In between the breakers, she swept salt water out of the kitchen door. Then she built a fire in the fireplace. When the room was fairly warm, she brought the others down.

Once their stomachs were filled, everyone cheered up a little—even dozed a while. But the day was a mixture of gratitude and discomfort. The house had withstood the onslaught, but its furnishings were soaked. Their food supply was dangerously low, and there was no relief in sight.

Abbie flew the flag at halfmast, with the hope that some ship, plowing through the rough waters, might think it a signal of distress and send some supplies to them. But they saw no ship.

In the days that followed, Mrs. Burgess kept to her bed, so Abbie was in full charge of the household and the lamps.

Though Lydia was willing to cook, Abbie was afraid she'd waste their food, and she wouldn't allow the younger girls to help her in the towers for fear they'd spill the valuable oil. She gave Lydia the task of attending to their mother's needs, and Esther and Mahala were to keep the kitchen clean and warm.

Abbie encouraged them all to carry on with their handiwork, and she tutored them and read the Bible to them every night. The busier she kept them, the less they complained about their hunger, for she now had to cut down on everyone's rations in order to stretch the food.

Throughout the days, she thought of her father. He'll come today, for sure, she'd tell herself each morning. He *must* come today. I'm so tired, and there's so little to eat.

The storm continued to rage for two weeks. The ocean never broke over the Rock again, but angry breakers pounded steadily, spraying the windows of the house. Abbie lost sleep and rest, but she kept on. If God would give her the strength, she would keep the lamps burning.

In mid-February, the ocean receded. Abbie opened the shutters, and for the first time in weeks, daylight flooded in.

A few evenings later, when she was up in the tower checking the lamps, Abbie noticed a tiny light offshore. She wasted no time getting down to the landing site. Her sisters soon caught up with her, and they all waited on the ledge.

A deep voice called out, "Ahoy there!"

"It's *Father!*" Abbie cried joyously.

"Father! Father!" the girls shouted as they scampered down the steps. Abbie caught the end of the rope he tossed and hauled the boat up on the ways. As soon as he touched shore, they rushed to him, chattering all at once.

He turned to Abbie and his voice choked. "I knew I'd find you all well and safe. Everyone in Rockland feared for your lives, but I told them this house would endure. And I knew you'd keep the lights burning, Daughter. They certainly welcomed me."

"Oh, Father, it's so good to have you home!" was all she could say.

That evening the family gathered at the fireside, relishing the fresh milk and fruit Mr. Burgess had brought. Abbie put away the other supplies, her spirits light again. Her father was home; their larder was full; and her mother had perked up a great deal already. Best of all, the granite house had weathered the storm.

According to the accounts her father brought from the mainland, it was one of the severest storms the oldtimers could recollect. It had wreaked terrible damage to the waterfront at Rockland, and there'd been word of many disasters on the high seas. Because of its deep drifts of snow, sleet, and gales, mainlanders were already calling it the "winter of the tempests."

After a while, Abbie sat down at the kitchen table and began a letter to Prissy. She explained some of the events of the past weeks, then added: "Though at times greatly exhausted with my labors, not once did the lights fail. Under God I was able to perform all my accustomed duties as well as my father's."

CHAPTER XVI

Benjy Comes Home

BEFORE SPRING CAME, Abbie could tell that 1856 would be an eventful year. The supply boat brought a pile of mail for Abbie. There were warm letters from Mrs. Haskell, Prissy, and other friends who'd prayed for their deliverance during their ordeal. There were notes from strangers, as far away as Boston and New York, commending her for her bravery and thanking her for her loyalty to the lighthouse.

News clippings described the damage the storm had wrought and listed accounts of heroism, including the story of Abbie and Matinicus Rock. Several ship captains, whose vessels had been lighted on their courses by Matinicus Light Station, banded together and sent a costly silver bowl fashioned by the Revere Silversmiths in Boston in recognition of Abbie's faithful service. But the most touching of all to her was the Friendship Quilt. A number of women in Rockland, many of whom she'd never met, had cut out various squares of cloth, embroidered them, and stitched them together into a handsome quilt. No two blocks were alike. Some had flower patterns, others were of birds, trees, seashells, or stars. In the corner of each block, the seamstress had embroidered her name. Knowing that appreciation and affection had been stitched into every square of the gift, Abbie cherished it.

In March, some officials from the Lighthouse Board came to the Rock to plan improvements in the service. In the three years since the Burgesses had moved there, fleets of coasting and fishing vessels, trading between the United States and the British Isles, had passed the Rock on their route. Though the steamship was still considered dangerous and expensive to operate, the officials believed that in time ocean steamers would be plying from ports such as Boston and Portland to Eastport and Halifax, Nova Scotia. With so many ships afloat, an efficient lighthouse on Matinicus Rock was of the utmost importance.

It was also believed that the tower lights shone out as far as fifteen miles, but various reports proved that the distance was nearer to nine miles. Moreover, the towers were situated too close together, for the lights appeared to blend into one.

Abbie's father learned that plans were afoot to erect new towers and to install new Fresnal lenses, which would provide a brighter beam. Engineers would be visiting the Rock before long to survey it and draw up specifications.

Abbie looked forward to the improved service the station could render to those who traveled this section of the ocean highway. But she was more concerned just then about the changes taking place in Rockland.

Mr. Pratt had predicted the building of clipper ships would slacken, and that had come to pass. The large number of ships in service, and the lack of sufficient trade to keep them all in use, had forced a lowering of freight rates, so that it was seldom profitable to keep the giant ships in operation.

Prissy wrote that with so much unemployment in town, her father's business was suffering. "So, Mama and I will have to forego some new clothes this year, until business improves. But I don't really mind—*too* much."

Spring came gently, luring the young girls to Rockland for more visits with their circle of friends. For Abbie, spring meant lobstering. She helped her father restore the old traps, and they made their usual repairs about the place. The work piled up so much that Mr. Burgess often spoke of Benjy and of how sorely his strong hands were needed.

"He'll come back one day," Abbie declared.

One evening in early May, scarcely two weeks after that conversation, Abbie saw from the tower a light waving near the landing site. She raced down to tell her father.

They set out for the landing with lanterns, speculating who it might be. It was too calm for a boat to run aground.

"*Ahoy there!*" a deep voice shouted, sending a shiver up Abbie's spine.

"Father, that's *Benjy!*"

"Not likely. We haven't heard from him in a month of Sundays."

But it was Benjy, waving to them from a small dory. Abbie was so happy that she burst into tears, and her father had a time keeping his composure.

The shadow Benjy cast in the light of the lantern, as he pulled the boat up out of the tide, showed he was taller than when he had visited them two years ago. As she embraced him, she could feel the width of his strong back.

"Oh, Benjy," she exclaimed, "we've missed you so!"

Abbie could hardly wait to see her mother's face. When the moment came, it was a joyous one.

"Benjy!" Mrs. Burgess cried, hugging him close. "My Benjy!"

The girls danced around, more sedately now, but as gleefully as ever.

Abbie and her mother dished up some supper for him, and they all gathered around, clinging to every word he spoke.

"You can set your mind at rest, Mother," Benjy began. "I won't be sailing away—least not for a long while. I've had my fill of fishing."

Mr. Burgess nodded. "I allowed you would one day, Son. It's a hard life."

Benjy regarded them solemnly. "I reckon it was Abbie, more than anything else, that brought me back. I was fishing off the Carolinas when I heard about the storm. We had some squalls down that way, but nothing severe. When we were passing near Boston, we saw where Minot's Ledge Lighthouse had been swept away.

"On the waterfront," he continued, "there was a lot of talk about the damage everywhere, and about the young girl who all alone kept the lights burning for so long on Matinicus Rock. I wanted to brag to everyone I saw that she was my sister. But I was ashamed to, for fear they'd ask me why I wasn't with my family when they needed me."

Abbie had a mind to cry. No matter why he'd come back, Benjy was home. Still, she daren't count on his staying—the sea would always be in his blood.

The younger girls were permitted to stay up late so they

could listen to more of Benjy's adventures. He'd been up and down the Atlantic coast several times and had souvenirs from every port.

There were no dolls in his knapsack this time. He had lengths of silk and lace, stockings and purses, and such things as the girls fancied now. He'd brought a book of poems for Abbie, as well as some embroidered linen napkins for her hope chest. A new pipe pleased his father, and Mrs. Burgess exclaimed repeatedly over her gifts of a rose wool shawl and brightly painted fan.

As though to prove his sincerity, Benjy went out lobstering with his father early the next day. Abbie had so much energy left at the end of the day that she read poetry and newspapers well into the night.

On Sunday afternoon, Benjy built a fire of old driftwood down near the cove and covered it with seaweed. Abbie laid a mess of clams and a great many lobsters on top, and put more seaweed over them. She spread a piece of old canvas sail over it all. Soon, steam began to rise, tantalizing them with its delicious aroma.

"This is the part I always hate about a bake," Mahala said. "The waiting and waiting."

Esther gave a sigh. "And the longer I smell the lobsters steaming, the more my stomach hurts."

Their parents came outside then, and they all sat around, basking in the warmth of the May afternoon. Bored from the waiting, the girls sang for a while, then listened to more of Benjy's tales, and, in turn, offered stories of their own about their visits to Rockland.

"I hope you're cooking enough this time," Lydia said to

Abbie. "Remember our last bake? Father ate four lobsters and Benjy five, and Esther had three all to herself."

Abbie smiled. "I added an extra one for each of us. You girls have grown so, you can probably eat as many as Father."

Presently, Benjy pulled up the corner of the canvas and poked through the steaming seaweed. "They appear to be ready. Here, Esther, take the first one. Don't burn yourself now."

He dropped a bright orange lobster on the rock at her feet. Esther tugged at it, finally tearing off one of its claws. "Oh, it's just right, Benjy."

Benjy handed the next one to Mahala.

The hour of waiting in the salt breeze had sharpened their appetites. They broke open the lobster shells quickly and pulled the succulent bits of meat away from the shells, licking their fingers as they did so. Forks were forgotten whenever the Burgesses feasted on lobster.

"Benjy, you should come home every week," Esther spoke up. "So we could celebrate with another lobster bake."

In time, Abbie was obliged to admit that the years at sea had matured Benjy considerably. His father was so convinced of Benjy's settled nature that he applied to the Lighthouse Board for an appointment for Benjy as assistant Keeper. In August, he was sworn in, and his annual salary of three hundred dollars began. In addition, the family would draw a double amount of quarterly rations.

Though Benjy was officially the assistant, he let Abbie light the lamps each evening. She took turns with him in cleaning the lamps and refilling them. But Benjy took over all the heavy work.

In June, a crew of men had landed on the Rock. They stayed several days to build an engine house and install the apparatus for the steam fog whistle. Now, during fogs, instead of pulling on a rope for hours on end, they had only to keep a fire going under a boiler and the whistle would blow intermittently throughout the day and night.

In late August, Prissy visited Abbie again. She was all aflutter about her engagement to a young lawyer she'd met in Boston. There were so many parties planned for her that Abbie's head whirled just thinking about them. She was pleased that her friend had found such happiness, but the distance between them was greater now than the expanse of water between the Rock and the mainland.

Prissy would be a young matron in Rockland and Boston society, hostessing dinners and parties, while Abbie wanted only to remain on the Rock and keep the lamps burning.

In December of that year—1856—the cutter again missed its call because of bad weather. Gales lashed the Rock for weeks, and snow frosted everything. Breakers splashed over the ledges, preventing any boat from landing.

Grateful as they were that the weather was not as violent as the winter before, the larder was emptying fast. Toward the end of January, the ocean calmed, and the temperature rose, renewing their hope that the supply boat would come. But days dragged on and there was no sight of it.

At supper one evening, Mr. Burgess announced: "I'm obliged to go to Rockland before the weather changes again. We'll be out of oil in another month and our food won't last much longer."

"I'm rightly the one to go, Father," Benjy pointed out. "You should stay here with Mother and the girls."

"You'll fare well without me, I'm sure. I'll be collecting my salary, so I can get the supplies. I've sailed in more foul weather than you, Son, so I'm the one to go."

It wasn't until her father put out to sea the next morning that Abbie realized how low their provisions were. Benjy rolled several hogsheads from the shed into the tower so that it would be handier to refill the oil cans. "These are the last ones, Abbie," he said solemnly, "so don't spill any."

Abbie stared at him. "Oh, Benjy, it might not last until Father returns!"

By nightfall, another gale struck with blustery winds and angry waves. It battered the ledges for several days, filling them with fear that last winter's calamity might be repeated.

After their father had been gone a week, Abbie told her brother privately, "Benjy, I'm obliged to cut down on our portions now. There's barely enough beans for two meals, and the smoked fish and other things are going fast."

"Stretch it as far as you can, Sis. There's no telling when Father will be back. All we need is a break in the weather—a couple of clear days—and he and the cutter will both be landing. Meantime, I'll stir up a fish—or a bird."

After another week, they were facing starvation. "I can't fathom what's delaying him!" Benjy paced back and forth in the kitchen as he talked. "The ocean's a mite rough, but seems to me he'd risk running aground to get those supplies back to us. Tomorrow," he declared, "I'll build a very small dory and set out for the mainland to look for Father. If I can't find him, I'll get some supplies and be back in two days."

"But why must you build another dory? What's wrong with the little dory in the boathouse?"

He met her eyes. "I daren't take it, Abbie, for if I don't come back—and Father doesn't return—you'll have to use the little boat to take the girls and Mother off the Rock. You can't stay here and starve. It would be smarter to try to make it to one of the neighboring islands and get food there."

"Then why don't you go to one of the islands?"

"Because it would be better to look for Father and the *Provider*—he may have it loaded with supplies and be stranded somewhere between here and Rockland."

No matter which way they imagined things were, the picture was grim. The only thing certain was that they needed food—and soon. After they told their mother their plans, she had a sinking spell, so Abbie put her to bed and had Mahala stay with her.

Abbie spent the following morning helping Benjy work on the dory he had started the day before. In the afternoon, she collected some old canvas and spent most of the evening sewing the pieces into a sail. Benjy moored the dory overnight, so it could swell and be seaworthy the next day.

Abbie got up unusually early the following morning to see Benjy off. She wrapped the last loaf of homemade bread, the cheese she'd been saving, and a baked potato, and put them in his knapsack. She served him a bowl of gruel, griddle cakes, and coffee. It wasn't really enough, but it was all she could spare.

At last, they lowered the dory, and when the breakers were just right, Benjy gave it a push into the water and jumped in.

Abbie held her breath as she watched the dory. It was lost from sight in the trough of a wave, but then reappeared for an instant before disappearing again.

She lingered on the shore, straining for another sign that Benjy was still afloat. When she saw nothing, she hurried back to the first tower. In the lamp room, she peered through a telescope, but there wasn't a sight of a boat in the clear gray dawn.

She sank down on the stool in the lamp room, her knees shaking. Dear God, she prayed, please let Benjy make it to land!

CHAPTER XVII

Abbie Keeps the Lights Aglow

"SOMETHING TERRIBLE'S happened to both of them," Mrs. Burgess moaned, as she turned her face to the wall. "It's been three days since Benjy left, and weeks since your father sailed. We'll starve, Abigail."

Abbie sat down on the bed and stroked her mother's hair. "God has not forsaken us, Mother," she said firmly. "He took care of us in the storm last year and He will see us through this. Why don't you sit in your rocker in front of the window —it's nice today."

She tried in every way to be cheerful, for the girls were as depressed as their mother. Abbie had been forced to cut down their daily amount of food considerably. As a result, the girls studied their portions and each of them compared her own with those of her sisters. She was glad that there could be no argument over the eggs. Each of the four hens laid one egg a day, and since Abbie's mother wasn't fond of eggs, the girls had one apiece.

The temperature dropped steadily throughout that afternoon, and by morning, the Rock was sealed in ice. After Benjy was gone a full week, the flour barrel was completely empty and the dried apples and raisins were gone.

Since her mother wasn't able to supervise the girls, Abbie was obliged to keep them busy. But each day they grew hungrier, bickered more, and worked less.

After a few days of this, she appealed to Lydia. "You're grown enough to be comforting your sisters. But you complain the most! Lydia, you and I have to be brave for the sake of the others."

Lydia tossed her head indignantly. "You're not fooling any of us, Abbie. You don't expect them back, either, long as the ocean's roaring like that. They'd rather let us starve than risk smashing a dory!"

"Lydia, what a dreadful thing to say!"

"I can't help it! I'm hungry—and I feel so *mean!*"

Abbie couldn't blame her sister, for she herself wanted to crawl into a corner and cry. Hunger had taken the edge off her patience, but she fought mightily to keep her senses. She had to face the situation squarely, and Lydia must, too.

"It isn't the rough sea that keeps them from sailing back, Lydia. It's the uncertainty of what they'll meet after they're well out on the water. Benjy's told me how dangerous it can be when ocean spray hits a boat and turns to ice. A boat can sink if the ice gets heavy enough. If we can just make the food last until the weather breaks, we'll do fine."

Each day she reduced the portions of food until they were subsisting on a daily ration of one egg and one cup of cornmeal mush apiece. It saddened her to see her sisters' wan faces. They were too weak to quarrel now, and sat huddled in front of the fireplace, wrapped in quilts.

Her mother fared better than any of them, for she lay in bed all day, and she'd thrived for many years on little food. Abbie discovered it was best to avoid her mother at this time. Much as she wanted to console her, she had to conserve her own strength for the twice-daily climb up the towers.

She knew that after the chicken grain was gone, the hens would no longer lay eggs. Whenever she thought of it, though, she'd remind herself of the delicious "Marblehead turkey" they'd enjoyed last Christmas, and her faith would be restored. She went outside every day to search for a fish that might have washed ashore. She tried to use her father's gun to shoot a sea bird, but gave up in despair over her clumsiness.

One evening, after Benjy had been gone for three weeks, she sat with her mother and sisters in front of the fire. They slowly spooned their pittance of mush, relishing every swallow as it slid down their throats to their empty stomachs.

"This is the bitter end, Abigail," her mother said. "If your father gets back before we starve, I mean to tell him that we're leaving this Rock——"

"Oh, Mother, please don't take on so! Father will be back. I've prayed so hard!"

"I know, child. So have I."

Hot tears splashed on Abbie's cheeks. She couldn't seem to stop them. Mahala began to cry, too.

"I don't like the lighthouse any more," Esther whimpered, "I don't like being hungry. It *hurts*."

Remembering Benjy's words about taking the others away from the Rock, Abbie considered it now. Perhaps it was best not to wait until the food was entirely gone. She'd take the hens with them on the little dory——

Just then, there was a lot of clattering on the kitchen steps. Abbie leaned forward, and her mother grabbed her arm, her fingers digging into the flesh.

"It's bound to be Father," Lydia whispered, getting up with effort. Before she could reach it, the door opened and their father walked in, carrying a crate. Behind him came Benjy with his knapsack bulging.

"Father!" the girls chorused, using their last bit of strength to greet him. At last, he came to his wife.

"We put out early this morning, Thankful, and it was rough going. We scraped ice off the dory all the way."

By then, Benjy had emptied the knapsack on the kitchen table. Out tumbled shiny red apples, thick loaves of bread, slabs of cheese and bacon, bags of cookies, and candies. The girls pounced upon the fruit and cookies, munching and smacking in pure pleasure.

Benjy brought in a jugful of fresh milk, and Abbie poured some for all. It was a joyous feast—a Christmas dinner in March!

While they stuffed themselves, the girls tried to describe to their father what it was like to be hungry. When it was Mahala's turn, she declared, "I couldn't sleep."

"You'll sleep soundly tonight, little one," Mr. Burgess replied, with a broad smile. Meeting Abbie's eyes, he added, "I reckon we all will."

They sat on in front of the fire, the mail set aside, while they discussed the weeks they had passed separately. Benjy told how he'd made it to the mainland and found his father, and then how the weather kept delaying them.

"I never worried so in my life," Mr. Burgess admitted. "I

thought the great storm was the worst that could happen, but this time—knowing how little food there was—well, I near about lost my mind."

"Oh, Father," Abbie broke in, "it's best we put it behind us. It was dreadful for all of us, but it's over now."

"And I aim to make sure it doesn't happen again," he assured them. "Two Decembers in a row the cutter couldn't make it, so I plan to make arrangements with the Lighthouse Board to have extra supplies brought out on the September trip—to tide us over the times bad weather holds up the cutter."

Despite the joy and relief of having the menfolk back safely, and plenty to eat, Abbie's mother sat quietly, staring into the fire.

"Sam," she said flatly, "I didn't hold to moving out here. It's no place to raise children. The work is hard, and it's lonely—and there's small reward for all the sacrificing. We're obliged to move back to the mainland before another winter comes—before something worse happens."

Mr. Burgess nodded. "Aye. You've a right to complain, Thankful, after what you've endured. But you've been out here so long you don't know all that's been going on in Rockland. They've had terrible epidemics all winter. Mrs. Haskell's nephew died, and Mrs. Stevens lost her baby—barely six months old."

"Mercy, Sam!"

"And just before Christmas," he went on, "a fire burned down a whole block of stores. They're still talking about last year's storm, too. Some women in Rockland had husbands out at sea last January—and they haven't heard a word to this day."

He looked at each one of them, his dark eyes solemn. "You all know that life's full of evils and dangers. It's best to take matters as they come, without complaining. You children will be faced with hardships of one kind or another all your lives. No matter where you live, or what you do, you'll be obliged to conquer fear. But it isn't hard, if your faith is firm—like Abbie's."

With all that had befallen them since they'd moved to the Rock, Abbie couldn't blame her mother for wanting to give up such a life. But she knew that her father was trying to teach them that they must face up to their responsibilities.

"Mother," she said gently, "we might as well stay on for as long as Father has his appointment. We've already weathered the worst that can happen to us. Now we know the house and towers will endure anything, and we won't let ourselves get so low on supplies again. I know the girls have complained at times about the life here, but it has brought us all pleasure, too."

CHAPTER XVIII

A New Keeper Is Appointed

IT TOOK some time for Abbie's mother to forget the misery of those weeks, but she perked up after the building got underway during April.

With the Rock so far from the mainland, the construction crew brought out materials every Monday and made camp on the Rock. While Mr. Burgess and Benjy were out lobstering, Abbie and her sisters cooked and served meals to the men. Their mother took great pleasure in neighboring with them, and there was daily progress for all to observe and discuss.

Over the months, new twin towers one hundred and eighty feet apart slowly rose from the rocky ground. One tower was placed about ten feet out from the granite house, the other one hundred and forty feet away. To protect the Keeper from the elements, a covered walk was erected to join the towers. Brighter lamps were installed—the lenses being changed from third-order to first-order. The former towers at each end of the granite house were cut down to its roof and became handy storerooms for the Burgesses.

Along with the new towers, a frame house, twenty-four by twenty-six feet, was built for the use of future assistants who might be married and need a separate dwelling. The girls took great delight in teasing Benjy about this.

When the smaller house was finally finished, Abbie's father decided that he and his wife would move into it and leave the granite house to the children.

"Your mother needs her rest," he explained to the others one evening. "I figure it'll be quieter in the other house, but we can have our meals over here together."

At first, the idea upset Abbie, for she'd never been separated from her mother. But she well knew how much better her mother fared when her surroundings were peaceful and quiet.

Tending to the lamps took more time and strength now, for there were nearly twice as many steps to climb in each tower, and there was the long walk from one to the other. Abbie continued to share the chore of cleaning the lamps and refilling them in the morning. She took pleasure in everything related to the lamps—but lighting them every evening was the joy of her day.

During the next three years, other changes came to the Rock. While Abbie looked forward to working about the lighthouse each day, her sisters daydreamed about life on the mainland. They debated so often with their father about the advantages of moving back to "civilization" that Abbie was worried he would yield to their wishes and resign his position.

At seventeen, Lydia was the prettiest of the Burgess girls. She had her heart set on attending an art school in Boston, and the Burgesses knew that she had just the spirit to do it and see it through.

Esther, now sixteen, and Mahala, who was fifteen, longed to attend a public school before they were much older. And Mrs. Burgess still missed having neighbors next door.

Just the thought of leaving the Rock threw Abbie into a panic. What would she do if they left here? How could she live without the lamps? She'd never rest for worrying over whether or not they were burning!

Before long, however, the approaching presidential election threatened the future of all the Burgesses. Abbie took a great deal of interest in the Democratic Party, since her father had aligned himself with it for many years. Now the young Republican, Abraham Lincoln, was gaining popularity, and Mr. Burgess feared he would be elected. If so, a Republican would be appointed as Keeper, and the Burgesses would have to leave the Rock.

"I hope Lincoln wins," Lydia declared one day when they were discussing it. "Then we can move—and we won't have had to make the decision."

"What will you do, Father?" Esther asked. "Where will we live?"

Mr. Burgess looked at his wife. "Your mother wants to move to Vinalhaven——"

"But that's just an island!" Mahala exclaimed. "It isn't the mainland!"

"It's land," Mr. Burgess said, "with soil to grow vegetables in and grass under our feet. We plan to take a small farm. There'll be plenty of people to be neighborly with and a school for you younger girls to attend."

Mahala glanced at her brother. "I suppose Benjy will join another fishing fleet."

Benjy shrugged. "Maybe. But if war breaks out between the States, I might join the Union Navy. I don't hold with using steam instead of sails, but it would be right exciting to serve on one of those steam gunboats."

With some anxiety they awaited the outcome of the 1860 election. A few days before the date, Mr. Burgess announced: "Some of the fishermen in town said they'd sail out near the Rock, after the returns are in, and give us a signal. If they fly a yellow flag, it means Douglas won. If the flag's white—we'll know Lincoln won."

Abbie's heart grew heavy, for she was sure that no matter how the election turned out, her father would soon resign, just to please her mother and sisters. But she supposed it would be selfish of her to object for they had a right to have the things that pleasured them.

The election was held, the fishermen appeared, and the flag they flew was white. Now they knew their father's appointment would expire in March 1861, so there was only one winter left to endure the isolation of the Rock. The other girls were deliriously happy, but for Abbie the weeks passed swiftly and miserably.

She could tell by the glances her father cast her way that he was concerned about her feelings. He spoke pointedly about the pleasure she'd find on a small farm, raising all the hens she liked and growing flowers.

"You're a young woman now," he reminded her. "It's high time you thought about marriage. You don't want to spend your life alone, or helping other women take care of their homes and children. After we move, you're bound to meet some fine young man you'll take a fancy to."

"Oh, Father, living alone wouldn't bother me. It's living without the lamps that grieves me. And being married wouldn't help at all——"

He patted her shoulder. "Aye. I know how you feel, Daughter. These years have brought me considerable satisfaction, too. But it'll sadden me if you take the loss so hard."

This was the closest Abbie came to saying what was in her heart. Even then, she wasn't sure her father really understood.

During the January thaw, he sailed to Rockland to collect his salary and buy more provisions. He returned with some interesting news.

"I know you all recollect that time I ran into Captain John Grant on the street in Rockland. That was months back, before the election. I allowed that I'd be losing my job if Lincoln won. Right then, I told John he ought to apply for the position. With his brood of sons, he'd have no trouble doing the work here. Well, he went right down to the Lighthouse Board and put in for Keeper.

"Yesterday," he went on, "I ran into him again, and he told me everything was all set. He'll be taking over the lighthouse in March."

"Well, I declare!" Mrs. Burgess brightened. "The Grants are moving here. I've heard you speak of Captain Grant, but I don't rightly remember the family."

Abbie swallowed hard. It was only a matter of weeks now. "Did—did you decide on the day, Father?" she asked. "We'd best be ready to leave on time."

He began to fill his pipe. "Captain Grant and I discussed you, Daughter. After I told him about all the work there is around the station, and how you set such store by the lamps, he suggested that you stay on for a while and show them the ropes. It would pleasure his wife to have your company. By that time, we'll be settled—and you'll be resigned to leaving."

Abbie's spirits lifted some. One more spring on the Rock would be a lovely memory to take with her. "If you gave your promise that I'd teach the Grants, then I'd best plan to stay."

⚓

CHAPTER XIX

Abbie Falls in Love

PACKING AND PLANNING filled the remaining weeks that the Burgesses lived on Matinicus Rock. They had collected so many possessions over the years that Benjy had to make one trip to Vinalhaven before their final departure. On the morning they left, they loaded Abbie's hope chest, most of her books, and her heavy clothes on the dory, leaving only what she would need for the spring. Her father calculated that Abbie would be there a month or so, but she overheard him tell her mother that Mrs. Grant wished Abbie would stay through the summer.

"That Mrs. Grant is a right neighborly woman," he said. "It'll do Abbie good to have someone fuss over her for a change."

It was a sad parting. Abbie hugged each member of the family tearfully, promising them she'd be along soon.

"Don't fret about me," she told her mother. "I'll be fine, as soon as I see the station's in good hands."

Abbie manned Matinicus Lighthouse alone for two days

and a night before the Grants arrived. She'd been told to expect them at about suppertime on the second day, so she fixed a fine meal and kept a lookout for a boat. After she had lighted the lamps, she glimpsed a light weaving about off-shore. Her heart began to pound. The Grants were here! She hurried down the long spiral iron steps and out of the door of the tower. She held her shawl around her with one hand and swung a lantern with the other.

When she reached the ledge, she stopped and tucked stray hair back into her braid. Then she went down the stone steps to wait until they were able to come alongside.

Her father had assured her that he'd explained to Captain Grant about the trick there was to sailing the boat in on a good wave, but Abbie wasn't sure he'd be able to do it the first time.

"Ahoy!" a man shouted over to her. "Would you be Abbie Burgess?"

"Aye!" she called back. "Welcome to Matinicus Rock!" She told them they must wait until the third breaker, then ride in on the crest of it. "Soon as you're in, throw me your rope and I'll pull the dory up on the ways."

She counted five people in the dusk and saw a heap of barrels and trunks. As soon as the dory neared the ways, one of the young men jumped out and waded up to the shore, the end of the rope in his hand. He was dark-haired and was wrapped in a jacket with a furry collar.

"A girl's got no call hauling such a weight," he grumbled as he passed her. She stood there in surprise, bristling a little while he pulled the boat in.

As the Grants climbed out of the boats, she could see they were all very sturdy people. After living with small-boned sisters and a frail mother, all of whom made Abbie think she was large and rather clumsy, she now felt small in the presence of the Grants.

Captain Grant was a huge man, huskier than her father. Mrs. Grant was stout, and their three sons were all big men.

"So you're Abbie Burgess!" the woman said, as she came over. "John, this is the girl we all heard so much about during the big storm back in '56." She drew Abbie against her bosom. "These are our sons," Mrs. Grant went on. "The oldest one's William—he's over there fussing with the barrels. Then there's John Francis. Next comes Isaac—he's the one who pulled the boat in. We have one more boy, Jarvis—but he's away in the Army. And if war breaks out, likely as not the rest of them will volunteer, too."

Abbie led them into the granite house and served the supper she'd kept warm. There was a ham, fried flounder, potatoes, biscuits, beets, stewed apples, three pies, and a pot of coffee. But even before she dished it up, she knew it wouldn't be enough.

"I didn't know your sons were all grown," Abbie said apologetically. "I'll fix something more."

"You'll do no such thing!" Mrs. Grant exclaimed. "Here— you set yourself down and enjoy your supper. I'll fix more food. All I've done this whole blessed day is rock in that boat. It'll be a pleasure to move about in a kitchen."

It was an unexpected treat to have someone else wait on the table. The Grants were talkative folk, and Mrs. Grant had a jolly laugh that cheered the whole room. Abbie listened in fascination to the men and answered the questions they asked.

Once she caught Isaac Grant studying her in a way that

flustered her. Now that he was close, she saw that he was quite handsome, with brown eyes that twinkled mischievously. In fact, he was handsomer than any of the young men she'd met the last time she'd visited Prissy.

Captain Grant asked pertinent questions about the lighthouse, and Abbie explained everything, which impressed them no end. The sons were interested in the prospects for fishing and how often the steam whistle had to be used.

"I don't blame you for being so upset about leaving Matinicus Rock," Captain Grant said after a while. "Once you come to love a certain way of life, it's pretty near impossible to change. If I weren't too old, I'd be out at sea. But I reckon this life is second to the sea."

Abbie smiled. "Father thought so, Captain Grant."

Captain and Mrs. Grant moved into the large bedroom in the granite house, leaving Abbie to keep the small one. The three sons took over the small frame house, but they ate their meals in the big kitchen with their parents and Abbie.

The Grants set about making the necessary spring repairs that first week. It pleased Abbie to see them so industrious. Every day, she took one of them around, explaining the workings of the lighthouse. She showed each of them how to operate the lamps and the steam whistle, and where each item was stored. She warned them of things that must be done in the event the weather changed.

Of all the sons, Isaac took the keenest interest in the lamps. The first day he climbed up into the towers with her, he plied her with questions.

"Now," he said, when they stood before the lamps, "teach me the tricks of the wicks."

Abbie laughed, blushing as she did so. She'd never known

a young man who could turn a phrase the way Isaac did. Yet, being around him made her strangely uncomfortable. Unlike the other Grant sons, who considered her a fixture of the lighthouse, Isaac paid her great attention, as though everything she said and did was quite important.

Abbie now found herself wishing that she were as pretty as Prissy, even though her mirror assured her that her own gray eyes and light-brown hair were not as plain as she had once believed. She was slender, too, and agile. For the first time in her life, Abbie cared more about her looks than about what the weather would be.

She felt so much at home with the Grants that she forgot, for a time, that her own loved ones were expecting her on Vinalhaven soon. The girlish giggles she was so used to had been replaced by the deep chuckles of young men. She stumbled over boots instead of sewing boxes; ironed shirts and trousers instead of ruffled petticoats.

Supper conversations were lively with political discussions. After Fort Sumter was fired upon, the Grant sons argued nightly about the pros and cons of enlisting.

In the evenings, Abbie usually slipped away upstairs with Mrs. Grant. While they sat with their sewing and knitting, Mrs. Grant would talk about the years her husband had been at sea, and how she'd had to raise the boys almost alone.

"After the Captain retired, we farmed for a while. We needed the boys' help, but we managed to keep them in school."

After years of nursing her mother, it was refreshing for Abbie to be with Mrs. Grant, who had such vitality and enthusiasm.

"My, we do get along, don't we, Abbie?" she said once. "I

wish you could live here with us. But that's selfish of me. Your folks are missing you, for sure."

Now that Mrs. Grant was mistress of the house, Abbie stood aside and let her do the chores as she pleased, offering help whenever it was needed. With so many hours to spare, she would stroll down to the cove at least once a day. Sometimes she just sat and watched the ocean; other days she would read. As the weather grew warmer, she took her hair down, letting the wind blow through it. Much as she enjoyed these times, she knew that each moment brought her closer to the day she must leave.

Soon, Isaac began to share her outings. At first, he just happened by and they exchanged pleasantries. Later, they shared picnic lunches and walks along the shore when the tide was out. He would open her poetry books and read them aloud to her.

"You're a strange girl, Abbie Burgess," he once told her. "You're sensitive, but strong enough to man a lighthouse. You read poetry—and haul in lobsters. For years all New England has been admiring your bravery, but you blush if a fellow touches your hand."

Abbie stammered, wishing she were as clever as Prissy, who always knew how to enchant a beau. "I—I don't know any other way to be," she said, "except the way I am."

He fixed his eyes upon her and said quietly, "Don't ever try to be different, Abbie. You're perfect now."

Isaac's brothers began to make remarks about the time he spent at the cove. "Must be a great place to fish," they teased.

Abbie enjoyed Isaac's friendship, but her thoughts were troubled. She'd dreaded to leave the Rock because of the lamps. Now, she'd miss Isaac just as dearly.

Isaac was as fond of the lamps as she; he felt the same sense of devotion toward them. She tried to console herself that this bond would ensure a lasting friendship, even after she left the Rock.

She fell asleep at night remembering the way he'd looked at her, and she awoke wondering if he would tend the lamps with her that day. Her father had predicted that she'd meet some fine young man, and Abbie was sure she had done so in Isaac Grant. One day she finally faced up to the truth. She must leave before she cared for him so deeply that she'd never be able to marry anyone else.

That very evening, she mustered all her courage and informed Mrs. Grant that the time had come. "I can pack tonight," she said, "and in the morning someone can take me to Vinalhaven."

Mrs. Grant's smile faded. "I hate to see you go, child. You know how fond of you we are. But I'm sure you've missed your kin. I'll let Isaac take you over in the dory——"

"Oh, no!" Abbie blurted, flustered now. "Please—not Isaac——"

Mrs. Grant smiled knowingly; she reached out and pulled Abbie close. "I know, child. Haven't I seen this flowering between you two? Isaac's so taken with you that he watches your every move. I heard him asking his father if he should marry—would he and his wife be allowed to have the little white house all to themselves."

Abbie gasped. "Sakes' alive!"

Mrs. Grant nodded, a twinkle in her eye. "I have a notion that if you go now and tell the Captain you want to leave tomorrow, Isaac will speak right up."

Abbie shook her head. "I—I couldn't, Mrs. Grant." She

moved over to a window and stared out at the tower lights glittering on the water. Her thoughts went back to the first evening she'd seen that view, eight years ago. "I'd best take a walk," she said, "and think for a spell."

She slipped outside, unseen, and headed for the cove. From there, she went down the stone steps. The tide was out, so she walked along the shore the way she had done so often. But she'd never had so much to think about before.

She knew Isaac liked her, but he'd given no sign that his heart was set on marriage. The thought of it thrilled her so much that it took her breath away. If she and Isaac were married, they could keep the lamps together——

Suddenly, she heard footsteps behind her. She whirled around. Someone was coming toward her. Her heart leaped when she realized it was Isaac.

"Abbie——" he called to her. In another moment she was held fast in the strength of his arms. Not a word passed between them, but the silence spoke more eloquently than any words could have.

He took her hand, and they walked together along the shore, admitting their love for one another, planning how they could be married and move into the little house.

"I must speak to your father right away," Isaac said, "and get his permission."

"We'd best go together, Isaac. Perhaps tomorrow."

Abbie had the joyous feeling that all her life she'd been sailing in one direction—to this place. All along, she'd felt the lighthouse was her duty, her destiny, and that God had led her here to do this work. Now she knew that He had also planned for her to share it with the man she loved.

Epilogue

Abbie Burgess and Isaac Grant were married in the summer of 1861, and remained on Matinicus Rock for fourteen years to help Captain John Grant tend the lights. During this time, they had four children—Francis, Malvina, Mary, and Harris.

After twenty-two years of faithful duty, Abbie left her beloved Rock to become her husband's assistant when he was appointed Keeper of Whitehead Light Station, Maine. While there, on August 7, 1881, Isaac made a "remarkable and gallant rescue" of two men who were drowning in the waters near Whitehead Light after their schooner capsized. For his heroism, the U.S. Lifesaving Service (now the Coast Guard), on January 31, 1882, awarded Isaac H. Grant a silver medal.

Abbie and Isaac retired from lighthouse work in 1890. Shortly before this, Abbie wrote a letter to one of her friends, which included these words:

"Sometimes I think the time is not far distant when I shall climb these litehouse stairs no more. It has almost seemed to me that the lite was part of myself. Many nights I have watched my part of the night and then could not sleep the

rest of the night, thinking nervously what might happen
should the lite fail. . . . In all these years I always put the
lamps in order in the morning and I lit them at sunset.
Those old lamps on Matinicus Rock—I often dream of them.
When I dream of them, it always seems to me that I have
been away a long while, and I am hurrying toward the Rock
to lite the lamps there before sunset. I feel a great deal more
worried in my dreams than when I am awake.

"I wonder if the care of the litehouse will follow my soul
after it has left this worn-out body! If I ever have a gravestone, I would like it in the form of a litehouse, or beacon."

Abbie passed away in 1892, at the age of 52. Her wish
for a gravestone was eventually granted. In 1945, historian
Edward Rowe Snow of Massachusetts, and his brother, poet
Wilbert Snow of Connecticut, conducted a public ceremony
at the gravesite of Abbie Burgess Grant.

Wilbert Snow read a poem he had composed to honor her,
and Edward Snow placed a miniature lighthouse—an alumi-
num scale replica of the one on Matinicus Rock—atop the
marker on her resting place. It was a tribute from grateful
citizens to the memory of a woman who had, for thirty-seven
years, unstintingly guarded the rockbound coast of Maine.